MAGGI KERR PEIRCE

A *Belfast* GIRL

A 1960s American folk music legend weaves
stories of a childhood on "the singing streets" of Ireland,
marriage in Scotland, and arrival in America

PARKHURST BROTHERS PUBLISHERS

Parkhurst Brothers Publishers

MARION, MICHIGAN

www.parkhurstbrothers.com

Parkhurst Brothers books are distributed to the trade through the Chicago Distribution Center, and may be ordered through Ingram Book Company, Baker & Taylor, Follett Library Resources and other book industry wholesalers. To order from Chicago Distribution Center, phone 1-800-621-2736 or send a fax to 800-621-8476. Copies of this and other Parkhurst Brothers Inc., Publishers titles are available to organizations and corporations for purchase in quantity by contacting Special Sales Department at our home office location, listed on our web site. Manuscript submission guidelines for this publishing company are available at our web site.

Printed in the United States of America

First Edition, 2013

2013 2014 2015 2016 2017 2018   12 11 10 9 8 7 6 5 4 3 2 1

Library of Congress Cataloging in Publication Data will be available on the publisher's web site when received from the Library of Congress

ISBN: Trade Paperback: 978-1-62491-017-3
ISBN: e-book: 978-1-62491- 018-0

This book is printed on archival-quality paper that meets requirements of the American National Standard for Information Sciences, Permanence of Paper, Printed Library Materials, ANSI Z39.48-1984.

Cover and text photos, for which the publisher expresses deep thanks, come from the author's family archive.

COVER DESIGN:
Wendell E. Hall

PAGE DESIGN:
Shelly Culbertson

PROOFREADERS:
Bill and Barbara Paddack

ACQUIRED FOR PARKHURST BROTHERS PUBLISHERS
AND EDITED BY:
Ted Parkhurst

THE PUBLISHER IS DEEPLY GRATEFUL TO:
Ms. Lee Ellen Marvin and Ms. Regina Carpenter

112013

This book is lovingly dedicated to my husband

Ken,

and our twin children,

Cora and Hank Peirce.

M.K.P.

ACKNOWLEDGEMENTS

Thanks to my husband of 49 years for putting up with the fancies of a creative woman whose breakfast cakes are few and far between.

Thanks to my longsuffering daughter, Cora, for her gentle help with an ancient mother who has yet to learn the intricacies of the personal computer, which seems to devour my texts without notice and hesitates to email the appropriate files to far-off folk.

Thanks to Terry Gross for interviewing me way back before she knew how much damage it would do her otherwise sterling reputation.

Thanks to Lee Ellen Marvin who dragged Ted Parkhurst to my house on a perfectly beautiful spring day when he should have been out of doors walking his Labrador retriever, or whatever it is that publishers do on fair spring days.

TABLE OF CONTENTS

A NOTE ON THE TEXT

It is an honor for Parkhurst Brothers Publishers to
present this charming memoir by Maggi Kerr Peirce.
While editing the text, we were reminded that Ms. Peirce
grew up in another culture, one that used a somewhat
different set of idioms than that of our American readers.
Some of her old country variants remain for charm
and authenticity, including some phonetic spellings.
Where reader comprehension was a concern,
we generally intervened as delicately as possible.
Any inconsistency or failure to achieve these editorial
goals accrue to our humble editor, not to the author.
We thank the gentle reader for understanding.

FOREWORD

No matter where you are in the City of Belfast when you raise your eyes, there will be the hills, everything from the stately Cave Hill with "Napoleon's Nose," the name given to a great outcrop of rock jutting forth from the precipice, to the homely hills on the other side of this red brick metropolis.

Beginning in the seventeenth century with a few houses at the mouth of the lough, Belfast grew by leaps and bounds to almost half a million inhabitants by the time I arrived on the scene in 1931. Ropeworks, linenhouses and shipbuilding enticed many country folk to better earnings and hopefully a better living. While most came from the interior of Ireland, many shipbuilders and their families emigrated from the ancient dockyards of Scotland.

In the 1930s I was known throughout my neighborhood as the small child who would announce upon meeting an unknown adult, "De ye know I was a wee prem?" At this early age I didn't even know that "prem" meant I had been a premature baby, but I knew it was something special. Born at eight months and a mere two lbs, my life hung in the balance for many months. Mother laid me in cotton wool, swabbed me with olive oil as my four year old sister, Dorothy, watched from a safe distance. At that time, my mother was 32 and my father 43 years of age.

To try to describe my family is an exercise in duality, for the simple reason that I belonged to two clans. The Walkers (my mother's family) and the Kerrs (my father's) were each an integral part of my growing up, but in dramatically differing ways. In all, there were twelve aunts, ten uncles (two in America) and twenty-one cousins. Of the cousins, three — Morrell, Derek and Jack — were our constant companions. They were like brothers. Dorothy and I were surrounded by love, strictness and total acceptance. When I became older, I marveled at this. A child takes everything for granted: a coal fire banked up the chimney, wholesome food on the table and a tidy home with a small back garden of four apple trees and six gooseberry bushes.

Our parents hid the world from us but we didn't know it. Both my sister and I were born during the Great Depression. Our father, who had been a Petty Officer in the Royal Navy, was released from his beloved warship the "Wahine." After the Great War, the only employment open to him was as a constable in the Royal Ulster Constabulary, the "RUC." As a policeman, he was dapper in his uniform and reliable in his duties, but poorly paid. Our mother, upon marriage, had of course to leave her job in one of the many small linen houses in the city centre to become a thrifty housewife. She did without many things so that we could wear good Sunday coats. While she insisted on showing a prosperous face in public by keeping two or three lovely dresses, she scrimped just where nobody would know: on her undies. Fine undergarments were terribly expensive in those days, so my mother made a very few sets last by darning and patching rather than going to the shop for new. Mother also made a simple pair of lisle stockings last a season by darning holes in the heels and toes. Her consolation — and ours, Dot and me — was that mother took us to an aged cousin, three or four times removed, a seamstress who made fine woolen coats for children. I can see mine today — I must have been about seven at the time. My new winter coat was a lightweight yellow wool with brown velvet buttons. And she made me a glorious hat of the same yellow wool, with a narrow brown brim. I wore the hat tilted away from my forehead to display my bangs, which we called "donkey fringe" in those days. The hat's brim was stitched with the same yellow as the coat, and accented with a brown ribbon, matching the coat buttons. Dorothy and I must have been insufferable, dressed for church in those special coats.

Mother kept our house shining. Her kitchen was the scene of many a plain dinner. Irish cooking wasn't much to speak of in those days, despite a wealth of fresh root vegetables. What my mother was celebrated for was her baking. Her specialty was cakes: coffee, chocolate, cherry, short bread, maid-of-honors, wee apple tarts with crème on top, and currant buns — delicious! Her recipes died with her; any inquiry of a recipe was dismissed with cupped hand gestures and pinched fingers, and fading phrases that began "Just a bit 'o…and a pinch of…"

Mother was focused on her children, her husband, and the house. Her economical household ways allowed her to pay off the mortgage five years early.

Daddy, being older and having seen the world, was full of stories, music hall numbers, ballads and street rhymes and songs. Mammy warbled hymns and popular songs from her girlhood. One of my earliest and sweetest memories was being carried up the stairs to bed with my head on Daddy's shoulders and my feet tucked under his oxter (underarm) with him singing "The Wee Filoree Man."

2

Mammy was not particularly religious but we all belonged to Bloomfield Presbyterian church. She took us there every Sunday. Daddy never attended nor did he need to. He had his own set of ethics. Mammy believed sanctimoniously that you "should turn the other cheek." Daddy thought that was poppycock and told us "If they can give it, they can take it." By the age of eight, I had accepted Dad's advice.

Looking back on my early days, what I most remember is that I would weep at the drop of a hat. My feelings were easily hurt. A teacher or aunt had only to admonish me for carelessness or poor spelling and I would become a sodden lump, dripping fat tears unto my polished shoes. Was I overly sensitive? As my dear Aunt Katy said in her broad Scottish accent, "Yer tear duct's aye near your ee." (Your tear duct is always near your eye.)

My big sister Dot could do everything well: darn socks, sew, paint watercolors, and draw designs. She wanted to become a writer. I imitated her with little success. I wasn't much good at anything and had not the foggiest idea of what I wanted to do. I was a typical baby of the family and went on my merry way. However, one thing I was interested in from the very beginning was collecting rhymes, sayings, and stories. I loved listening to old people as they told interesting facts and legends. The grown-up girls (two or three years older) passed on skipping rhymes and walking songs. These I lapped up like a starving kitten. I remember writing down an unknown counting rhyme from a girl called Sadie Shaw. She was from the country. We were both seven. Her rhyme went "One potato, two potato," and I'd only heard, in our neck of the woods:

Eeny meeny minney moe;
Set the baby on the po.
When she's done,
Clean her bum.
Eeny meeny minney moe.
Yer OUT!

By the age of fourteen — and after a stint at a Business College where I learned shorthand and typing — I was out working a 44 hour week in a hemstitching company's office. Within a year, I also had discovered the Youth Hostel Association and the joys of mountain scrambling and hill walking in the Kingdom of Mourne, some thirty miles south of the city. We were an adventurous crowd. In the years after the Second World War (1939 – 1945) many young people all over the British Isles immigrated to Australia, America, Africa and Canada. Dot and I traveled and worked in Northern Europe. We were casting off our homeland and, like Dad, "seeing the world" with rucksacks on our backs and big boots on our feet. We lived in Sweden and Holland, roamed in Finland, Norway, Denmark and Germany, learning languages. In Sweden, we worked in a chocolate factory before moving on to Stockholm where we washed dishes in a swanky restaurant. Months later we could be found sewing buttons on coats in Amsterdam. Our adventure came to a sudden halt when Daddy took very ill. We returned to Belfast to see him breathe his last. Then we started again to work in our home city.

3

Dorothy and I eventually found ourselves working in Edinburgh, Scotland, and after several years she went traveling to India and Pakistan. I met Ken, my American husband, in the Unitarian church through a mutual friend. We were married at St. Mark's under looming Edinburgh castle. In America we live half a mile along the road where Ken was reared. After two years in this country and with bonny twins, I took on the task of running the Tryworks Coffee House. My tenure lasted for twenty of its thirty five year life in First Unitarian Church in New Bedford, Massachusetts. It was at this time, when I was opening the minds of my Tryworks kids to the folksongs and music of the British Isles, I began to be asked to perform in Folk Festivals. First, I performed at our Coffee House in New Bedford, Massachusetts. In 1969 I was invited to sing at the Open Circle at Newport Folk Festival by Frank Warner, one of the great folk music collectors. He and his dear wife Ann and I became fast friends later on, and I performed at many festivals all over America and Canada. This was during the turbulent 1970s.

Dr. Kenny Goldstein, British Isles folklorist at the University of Pennsylvania discovered that I could tell stories and recite rhymes I had heard as a child. He finagled me into gathering all my street chants, songs and parodies into a manuscript that became *Keep the Kettle Boiling,* a book first printed in America. Soon, it was published in Belfast to great fanfare by Appletree Press. I even met the Lord Mayor, a lovely man with a glorious gold chain.

In 1976 at the age of forty five, I passed my GED and was accepted at our local University (then SMU but now University of Mass. at Dartmouth). I majored in German. After a brief respite, I returned in 1983 to finish with a degree in Art History. I enjoyed every minute of it. In my last semester, I wrote a short story which was chosen as best in class. I had never written before, but liked learning to read as a five year old, as soon as I found out I could, nothing held me back. Thereafter, reading my stories became part of my performances.

Returning in memory when, as a youth I picked up almost by osmosis, songs, chants, recitations and yarns of my family — especially my Aunt Aileen Murphy — and from the street, I find myself lost in a cloud of bewilderment. How and why did all of this material stick to me like Velcro? Perhaps it was just meant to be, as simple as that. I hope I have passed on, in my writing, singing and performance, the way of life I inherited as a child and girl in a city that, within a few years after my leaving would be decimated by sectarian violence. I want people to know that in Belfast, life had not always been violent. I find that it falls to me to tell the tale.

M.K.P.
March, 2013

Orange Billy, the family cat, with Maggie Kerr Peirce, Easter, 1932.

STORIES
FROM
MY LIFE

THE LARGE STUFFED RABBIT (1937)

Money was as scarce as hen's teeth when I was a child in Belfast, but tradition dies hard, and the year I turned an adorable six — dark hair cut in a fringe and eyes larger than my face, my Mother, blessed be her memory, resolutely put aside sixpence a week in order that Margaret, Her "baby" as she lovingly called me, could have a studio photograph taken.

The days had not yet arrived when fond fathers would present Polaroids for Christmas (or any other time, for that matter), so on the morning of the big event I was put through my paces like a year old colt. My hair was transfixed with curling irons into tight biddable curls and then brushed until my scalp tingled. My patent leather shoes, button-hooked across my instep, were wiped with olive oil until they glistened and my eyebrows, forever unruly, were licked into shape by a well-aimed flick of Mammy's spittled wee finger.

Over my liberty bodice, slip and hand-knitted knickers my slim body was engulfed by my party dress of green organdy with frills below the waist and tight yellow, pink and blue flowers bunched at intervals above my belly button. In order to keep this pristine and glowing picture unruffled by wind, splatter or downpour, my Mother spent her money on a tramfare to Mountpottinger, a mere two miles away. This journey would normally have been made on foot. It was where the Holywood Studio — "Every Portrait a Charmer" — was, and it was renowned in the neighborhood as the place to have your likeness taken.

Off I skipped with Mammy, my shoes squeaking on the pavement, hair bobbing wildly, and still smelling slightly of scorched ends. I was agog with excitement. We climbed the narrow stairs to the studio. My heart beat like mad. .

Mr. Heggarty, ("He's not a Catholic, Billy," Mammy had said to Daddy the week before, wishing to nip in the bud any idea that she was handing over his hard-earned Protestant cash to one of "the other persuasion") met us at the door and ushered us in. He sat me upon a raised platform and thereupon disappeared behind his camera under a welter of black cloth. I was fascinated. I was nervous. When I am nervous I eat my nails. Mammy admonished me loudly. I felt irritated by my Mother and hung my legs over the edge of the chair like dead turkeys in the butcher's window. Mr. Heggarty appeared from behind the black cloth and cautioned me with a "Now, now pet, you must cross your ankles neatly; no nice little girl hangs her feet over like that." I scowled in his direction.

Again Mr. Heggarty's head appeared. This time he had had a thought. "Margaret," he said, "come with me into the next room and let me show what I have for you". Obediently I slipped off the chair and followed his stooped figure. In the corner, resting on two stout legs was the largest stuffed rabbit I had ever seen. He was as tall as me. His pale grey body had a bib of white, and he had the sweetest pink nose from which sprouted bristling white whiskers. I was entranced, and had to be led back to my pose by Mr. Heggarty who said, "Now if you are a good wee lassie, I'll give you that bunny to take home with you".

I was so good! I could not do enough for Mr. Heggarty. I smiled brightly toward his shrouded form, crossed my ankles neatly with the tiniest creaks from my oiled shoes and pointed my fingers, just so, on each side of my frilled skirt. The flash bulbs popped three times. On each occasion I showed my sharp little teeth in the most charming of smiles and held my pose like the good little girl I wasn't. "Wonderful, wonderful, Mrs. Kerr" said Heggarty, "what a grand wee daughter you have there, do you want the picture framed, three shillings and sixpence and call for it next Wednesday?" With these words he hustled us down the stairs and into the street thronged with home-going workers.

"But he forgot to give me my rabbit, Mammy". I looked at her, totally bewildered; I'll run back and get it." There was an embarrassed cough from my Mother. "Darlin'," she said, "he didn't mean it." 'But Mammy," I said, "you know that you never break a promise." Again an uncomfortable pause. "He only promised you the rabbit so that you would sit still and stop fussing; it was just a ruse honeybun to get what he wanted from you." I gazed up at my Mother unbelievingly. A grownup did not mean what he said? A promise was not really a promise? Even a penny ice-cream cone, liberally spotted with raspberry cordial, did not cheer me up.

The adult world had been found wanting. In my heart there was an empty space that should have been filled by a large grey and white stuffed rabbit with the handsomest of whiskers. Slowly I trudged homewards, tears coursing down my face and salting my ice cream cone. Gone were my glittering shoes, now dust smeared. Gone was my curling hair, now slowly unwinding in the damp evening air. Panic-stricken, I realized that the outside world was filled with peril. I inhabited a world of promises not kept and principles not upheld.

For once Mammy, usually short-tempered about crying in public, held my hand tightly and kept saying "Augh, my wee birdie, always remember:

> Love many, trust few
> Always paddle your own canoe".

I didn't understand what she meant until many years later.

THE LUCKY PACKAGE

The format was invariably the same. On the Fridays that Daddy was free from his police work, Mammy and my sister Dorothy and I would journey into town and see the latest movie. Daddy was patience itself and always allowed our Mother to choose, so therefore my childhood was filled with weepy, Ethel M. Dell-type films, as Mammy was of the sort who never believed she had enjoyed herself unless a handkerchief was wrung to a sodden, tattered rag by the end of the performance.

On one such afternoon, my parents met us at the gates of North Road School to find me dancing with excitement. Somehow that day I had won Miss Moore's weekly lucky package, a gift only conferred upon the good or the brilliant. I was neither of these. On the day in question, there I stood proudly waving a pink paper bag, sealed at the top and loudly proclaiming in large hand lettering, "Lucky Package — a bundle of surprises" on its side. I knew there would be conversation lozenges with such titillations as "Kiss me quick" or "You are a perfect peach" stamped on their chalky surfaces. But what thrilled me more than anything was the unknown prize that was sure to be lying in the bottom of the bag.

Being of the type who always eats her marzipan last off my portion of Christmas cake, I carefully carried my reward un-opened and un-examined unto the tram, and just as painstakingly climbed down from that vehicle and thence to the Imperial Picture House, gleefully hugging myself in anticipation.

Unfortunately, my Mother, who was of the Old Brigade, and believed that not only should children be seen and not heard whilst the film was in progress, directed a loud sshhh when I tried to rip open the package. We had arrived just as the big picture commenced. Seating herself on my right, Mammy quickly lit up a cigarette and puffed happily as the strains of sobbing violins heralded "The Barretts of Wimpole Street." As was usual with these weekly cinematic jaunts, the story was far above my six-year-old head. I watched a woman on a sofa consumed in a fit of the vapors, a father thundering demands, and a poetic young man, whom I presumed to be the hero, promising undying devotion — all with total delight and complete incomprehension. Daddy, sitting on my left and oblivious to Miss Moore's prize bag I held in my lap, slipped me half of his chocolate bar. Appreciation warred with frustration as I nibbled squares of chocolate, still fingering the mystery prize of my lucky package.

The bagged object seemed to be quite long and slim. I wondered if it might be a little pen. Nobody in my class had a fountain pen. Actually we hadn't learned to write in ink yet, but I rather coveted my father's tawny brown pen. On the other hand, it might be a game, or better still, a tiny flag which would burst into a million colors when swirled about the head. I squirmed in happy expectation. What might it be?

The screen was flickering slightly, mottled by black dots reminiscent of the pepper on my potatoes which Daddy always insisted on giving me. He swore that black pepper cleared the head. Somewhere along the row of seats, a woman sobbed brokenly. I peered through the gloom, but could only decipher that it was neither my mother nor my sister. That was a relief. I sat further back in my seat and surveyed my woolen stockings. They were wrinkled across the knees like an elephant's behind. I surreptitiously hitched them flat by pulling them up through the pockets of my coat. My mother gave me such a poke in the ribs I near lit on the floor. "Be at peace, can't you," she hissed, "don't annoy the devil out of the folks around ye." I pouted and lay on the seat, so that my head leaned crookedly on the lower portion of the back, whilst my licorice-legs spiraled in front of me, where they suddenly hit the docile pair of shoes sitting there. The owner turned round and tut-tutted at me. Instantly, I was hauled up by a mighty heave of Mammy's irate arm. Cowed, I sat stone still and stared at the screen.

The film story had hit its peak of pathos. The daughter was leaving her father's house forever. Not knowing this, the father lectured his invalid daughter with a doleful countenance. A manly tear bejeweled his stern eye. I could hear Dorothy snuffling nearby. There was not a dry female eye in the whole cinema.

It was at this juncture that I finally succeeded in wiggling the prize from my pink package. Squinting at it in the darkness I could dimly make out the shape of a cigar. I turned toward my father, who was delicately holding his Player's cigarette poised in his right hand. I swiveled toward my mother, whose cigarette (A Gallaher's Blue, as both parents were loyal to their own particular brand) was glowing like a fuzzy beacon, and slowly I lifted the toy cigar to my lips.

I sucked. Nothing happened. I blew in the other direction. A noise, half way between the gasp of a dying cow and a wail of a sick banshee, raspberried through the picture house. For one moment there was an electrified silence as people tried to associate the honk with the soul-stirring speech issuing from the silver screen. The next instant my father, habitually the soul of discretion, slapped his thigh and with an enormous guffaw of laughter, kicked his heels in the air. All up and down the packed rows of the Imperial, people — who a moment before had been weeping copiously — roared with laughter, until their tears of merriment far outweighed their celluloid-induced grief.

Fortunately for me, the film was almost at its end, and as it was such a dark film, nobody could quite ascertain where the squeaking bray had originated, so that I was able to creep from the cinema, head hung in shame and tears tripping me. Nothing that either Daddy or Mammy said could quite calm me. Daddy chuckled and even Mammy saw the joke, without the usual social implications of bad manners. But it didn't matter. I sobbed brokenly all the way to Castle Junction where we caught our tram. My feelings — the feelings of a six-year-old girl — had been hurt. I felt that I had made a fool of myself and the whole cinema, nay the whole world of Belfast, had laughed at me. I scuffed my toes in the gutter and moped my way up the twanging-metal stairs of the homebound tram.

For once Daddy did not sit beside Dorothy, his favorite, but jostled me in by the window. I snuggled in the arched safety of his arm as the conductor rattled up the stairs and rang our tickets with a ping! ping! ping! ping! for each of the Kerr family.

Daddy squeezed my shoulder and said "You know, chickabiddy, that today reminded me of the time I sat on the Minister's hat."

Immediately I sat up. "What?" I giggled, "You really sat on a Minister's hat?"

"Yes," said Daddy, "and to make matters worse he was praying on his knees in the middle of the kitchen at the time. Everybody in the house laughed, including dear Pastor Willoughby, God rest his soul, but you know, I thought they were laughing at me, and do you know daughter mine" — here he paused and opened his eyes wide and gazed at me in feigned astonishment, "even though I was a boy, I almost cried. I definitely remember a big lump in my throat" he added. "My family, you see, were only laughing at the situation, the way the folks in the picture house did today — both your cigar-tooting and my hat squashing were accidents. Do you understand what I'm getting' at, honeybun?"

Dumbly I nodded blinking my sticky eyelashes. I definitely did feel more cheerful by the time our tram finally reached Irwin Avenue. Setting out on foot then, I curled my hand into Daddy's long-fingered smooth one and jauntily we strolled along. Mammy and Dorothy hurried on before us so that the fire would be roused and the sausages frying by the time the man of the house arrived home. Daddy and I took our glorious time.

We looked at one another and smiled. Taking my cigar from my pocket I placed it to my lips and blew several penetrating blasts. A flock of pigeons pecking by the breadman's horse and cart rose with a great flapping of wings. Daddy and I stood and watched them in the waning light, rising and wheeling in the air above. Then we looked at one another again, and laughed and laughed and laughed.

THE MOST BEAUTIFUL DOLL IN THE WORLD

My Mother, who usually wore a small twisted smile bravely affixed to her face in public, was at heart a sad, unsettled person. Not until the days when my sister and I had grown up and gave her to understand that her thoughts were sound and highly admirable (when she had been led to believe that she was alone in a world that not only didn't understand her, but that she had never really comprehended) did her face slip into its natural repose of anxious sadness., However, it was because of this particular expression, seen often at home, that I loved my doll Kathleen best of all.

For on Kathleen's paper mache face was mirrored the same look of intense loneliness, and for all her pretty features, rounded lips and retroussé nose, it was this expression of inner unhappiness that made me love her with a passionate devotion that none of the other celluloid dolls in my collection ever kindled in my seven year old breast. Kathleen was a lady doll, with blonde frizzed hair ironed into corrugated waves. She wore a short dress of indeterminate style and on her sawdust stuffed feet thin white socks and black canvas shoes.

Whenever I wheeled my pram in the street I would always take Kathleen, which proved rather difficult as she could not sit up, being unbendable. She would either be propped in a diagonal manner with a pillow supporting most of her back, or lie, tucked in from head to toe looking like the Egyptian mummy in the Belfast Museum, with only her tragic wee face peering in a concerned way at the overhead clouds. Neighbors would stop me during these perambulations, as older people were invariably kind to small, would-be mothers. They would shower praises upon me, "Augh, isn't she lovely dear, what's her name, she's the spit of her mammy," "Is this the new baby, well doesn't she look nice?" "Takin' yer latest wee wean for a dander, pet?" And to all of these good people I would nod happily and trot on my maternal path, pleased with the world for praising my Kathleen-of-crimped-hair.

One day I was to play with my friend Aileen Graham up at the top of our street. Thinking I might appear snobbish to use my pram (it was not every little girl who had a pram) for such a short distance, I bundled my dear Kathleen in a square of old blanket Mammy had given me and pattered off to spend a happy time playing "Houses" with Aileen, both of us taking turns to be the Father, heavy-footed and judiciously paternal. However, upon arriving at the Graham household, I could hear hoots of laughter issuing from the yard next door. Mrs. Graham told me that Aileen had gone there to play with the Magees. "Tell her that there'll be a piece of currant soda and a glass of milk for you both, as soon as I dress the baby", she called after me. I slowly lifted the iron latch on the Magee's gate.

Some kind of rowdy game was in progress with all the Magees, a pale skinned country family, who was not only marked by their accent but also with the gusto with which they attended a local Gospel Hall. One could see them, every

Sunday, in creaky black suits walking soberly down the streets with bibles the size of tea-trays under their arms and exuding such an air of self-righteousness it made the very hedges tremble. Now the boys were hurling themselves on one another in complete abandon, hallooing and caterwauling, making Eva, the only sister, and Aileen shriek and laugh and run around the gooseberry bushes and leap over the vegetable beds.

I stood shyly, wanting to speak to Aileen but not daring, clutching Kathleen to me and waiting for the powerhouse of high spirits to run its course. Instead, the flow of boys wheeled in my direction. Walter, the youngest, who I always felt was a little soft in the head (though in adulthood he became a serious and resplendent Elder in his wife's church) caught sight of the intruder. With a whoop, utterly untinged by mercy, he bore down upon my quaking form. I smiled bravely and said "Hello Walter; can I play?" His mouth, filled with uneven strong teeth in short pink gums opened in a roar. Snatching my beloved bundle from my arms, he yelled, "Yoops, look at the baby," and into this frenzied mob he flung my straight little lady-like Kathleen.

First, she was whipped from hand to hand. I ran into the fray trying so hard to catch my dear doll as she plummeted to earth. Invariably before I could quite reach her, nail-bitten fingers would catch her again and send her indomitable slim form high up to the blue sky. Without hesitation, I would run to where she would descend and throw my arms up. Once again, gangling youths would seize her by the legs, poke her wispy hair into my face and sneer, "Can't you catch her, here, here!" As my short legs would again pump toward her, up she would be thrown, boys' laughter and shrieks growing in volume.

By this time, the tears were blinding me. Jagged, angry sobs were shaking my body. Tom Magee, the one most inclined to kindness, suddenly saw my plight. Pushing my doll at me, he shouted, "Quick, quick, away home!" In a blur of tears, I grasped my Kathleen and ran down the hill to the safety of Mammy's lap and the comforting smell of her face powder.

"That crowd of scittery gits," my mother hissed (a git, in local parlance, something of an unkempt person, and scittery was an adjective meaning scat). Although she was mild of manner with other people, she could give full rein to a salty tongue at times. "There, there pet, let's look at your baby." Eyelashes in wet spikes, I held Kathleen up. Her dress was only a few tattered bits of finery. Both shoes were lost and one of her legs leaked a fine trickle of sawdust. Worst of all was her face. Her hair stuck in tufty yellow whorls from her head where much glue had given way and her dear sweet nose was no more. "Oh Mammy, look at her wee nose; it's gone!" I screamed. On seeing my sister returning from school, I sprang to her, telling her the whole story in a breathless, sobbing monotone. "Don't worry, Margaret," said Dorothy, "Those Magees are nothing but a bunch of louts. I'll fix her nose as good as new." But of course she didn't, she couldn't.

That evening my big sister shaped some glitter wax into a pale pink nose and formed it on top of the remainder of the old one. It gave Kathleen the look of a lady of easy virtue. Who drank. Her nose glowed like a beacon in the center of her sad little face. I loved my dolly all the more fiercely, and profusely thanked Dorothy for the fine nose job.

Never again, except in cold courtesy, did I speak to any of the Magees and I politely refused invitations to Aileen Graham's.

Once bitten, twice shy.

THE HAUNTED HOUSE IN EVELYN AVENUE

My Great Aunt Annie lay in bed in her front parlor for all the years of my childhood. They lived in Lomond Avenue, a stone's throw from our house. Being, at that time, filled with Band of Hope charity, which was dinned into you in Northern Ireland morning, noon and night, I was of the opinion that it was my Christian duty to visit my 70 year old invalid great aunt every week.

In retrospect, I never knew whether she was really ill or merely wished to escape the attentions of Great Uncle Willie. He was a man to be reckoned with. Huge of stature, mighty of voice, he reminded me then and reminds me still of what a man should look like. Never had I seen such a fine, dome-shaped head, a figure of such grandiose proportions, or such thick lips gripping a penny cigar between long curving teeth. He had been said to be "quite a man for the ladies" and perhaps Great Aunt Annie had just "retired" herself to the front room, where she lay in bed-jacketed splendor, carefully combing her pure white hair, watching the world pass by with the aid of a mirror she held in her hands. She rather resembled the "Lady of Shalott," I used to think during my poetic period.

Great Aunt Annie must have been somewhat amazed at the dutiful visiting routine of her nine year old great niece. During one of our afternoon conversations, she told me the full story of the haunted house in Evelyn Avenue.

"D'ye ever walk round by the haunted house?" Her eyes glinted through her gold-rimmed spectacles. As it was the only real haunted house in the neighborhood, beside several houses that merely lay empty, as the Depression was not long over, I nodded my head. In my most wheedling tone I drew nearer. "Tell me what really happened. Mammy won't tell me, you see though she always orders me not to look up at the window at the back."

"Ah, no wonder child". Her voice sank lower. "Is the place still lying vacant? Have you ever gone in?"

"Oh no, Aunt Annie, but I've peeped in at the staircase a couple of times.

"Aye, the staircase, *That's the one, the very one.* Sure it happened to me when I was only a young bride. You see when Great Uncle Willie and I were newly married we lived on Evelyn Avenue near the handsomest, richest house in the whole district. 'T'was the one near the railway line. There was a backyard, you know, where they could stable a horse. Inside, the house was said to be lovely. The father of the wee boy, the one you've heard of, was well to do and he spared nothin' for home nor wife. Unfortunately, only after a couple of years and the one wee son, his wife up and died. Like many a man before him, he married soon after. Remember the old saying, "Marry in haste, repent at leisure." Here Aunt Annie broke off her tirade and shook her finger warningly at me, and I nodded to show that I'd remember.

"Well, as I was saying, he married this second woman while the wee nipper was still a toddler, but seemingly nothing that that poor child did could please the stepmother. When the father would come home after a hard day's work, his new wife regaled him with the villainies of his young son. Over the next few years, his son grew to hate his stepmother. The wee boy went out of the way, childish and temperamental as he was, to be as annoying and naughty as possible.

Yet the neighbors agreed that the boy was a sweet-natured child, a model of youthful demeanor. Forbidden by his stepmother to play with any of the other children in the street, he could be seen waving at passersby from the back upstairs window, fair hair curling around his wee head. Still, it was frequent that when the father arrived home, he would chastise his son for the things the boy's stepmother reported he'd done. As the months wore on, the child and the stepmother wrangled and quarreled, as only people who live closely can. The father became so distraught with this never-ending complaining and screaming that he would take his belt off and thrash the child blue and purple. We neighbors would stand and listen to the son's wails and say to one another how hard the father was wi' his poor wean.

"But y' know," said Great Aunt Annie, "In those days they didn't have the NSPCC and even if they'd had we believed in taking care of our own and minding our own business. Many's the night as I hastened round the back entry of the house I would hear that young one crying "Daddy, don't — Daddy don't," and the roar of rage that man would give. I was sure it would take the very heart out of me, especially as I was carrying my first myself by that time."

Then one night, a bitter cold winter one it was, the child must have done something dreadful. I think left the yard gate open and the horse bolted, something like that. Well, the next door neighbor who I knew well in those days — she's long since dead and gone, God rest her soul, said that the crying and sobbing started after the child had been put to bed. From what she could see, peering through her curtains from the other side of the street, the father dragged the boy downstairs and proceeded to whip him beyond all reason. Had the distraught father lost his mind? The child struggled to drag himself up the stairs. At the top he battered with his wee fists on the window, shouting "Help me! Help me!" Nobody came because, you see, in those days none of us ever crossed the threshold of a home to interfere in a family matter.

"And did he die?" I asked, well knowing the answer. "Yes, Margaret, that he did. The men in the district said that it was his second wife's fault for being a shrew and forever complaining. They said that it should be a lesson to us. But we women and girls wept because we hadn't had the courage to put a stop to it. We knew, you see that the last dreadful beating had not been the first one by a long chalk, and, after all, the child had been his father's flesh and blood. We could forgive neither the crone of a stepmother nor the weak father who beat his own son.

For a while, Great Aunt Annie lay silent. As if to herself and looking past my small form into the reaches of that clock-ticking, stuffy room, she continued. "You know they tried to sell that house afterwards. It was a lovely house, spacious and gracious. Many a family came along to look at it — it being near the railway and close to the shopping district. But within one week of it being up for sale, groans and screams were heard from that house in the nighttime. Many folk, your Uncle Willie included, swore they saw a young fair-headed lad at the upper window — the one at the top of the staircase. Some people even moved away saying that the place had become unholy.

Then the realtor sold that house to a large family, and we thought that would put an end to the horrors.

Great Aunt Annie paused. "It didn't though. The new family had barely placed the furniture in the ground floor, and the curtains hung, before the weeping and cries continued. No matter how much the wee skivvy, the wee country girl they'd brought with them to help with the housework, scrubbed the marks on the stairs, the stains would be back the next day. It was said the girl gave in her notice within a week. Although the man of the house had the whole place re-decorated he could do nothing with the floral wallpaper in the hallway and up the stairwell. Small bloody handprints would show through the paper, little thumb marks, smaller than your own Margaret. I saw them myself. Little hands, almost like a baby's.

Well, that family I was telling you about, they up and left. Then another lot came and then they left too. It was always the same story. Dragging of small feet on the stairs, screams during the night, and always the delicate handprints on the wall. Eventually, the realtor had to give up the idea of selling the place. There the house lies — derelict to this day.

That was the story Great Aunt Annie told me years and years ago. Some ten years after she told me this story, housing was short in Belfast because of the German bombing. There was talk of reconditioning the house in Evelyn Avenue. But the powers that be, in some pokey, file-lined room in City Hall, again considered the history of this place. Instead, in the 1950s it was quietly leveled to the ground and an electric power house built in its place. Even solid Belfast city-planners knew that there was no good to be gained by ever building again on evil ground.

Maggi Kerr Peirce performs at the 1969 Newport Folk Festival with her twins at her side.

At Grandpa Walker's house, Finaghey, Belfast, 1931, Infant Maggie and sister Dot.

Maggi, cousin Jack, and sister Dorothy in Belfast, 1936.

Maggie Kerr Peirce performing at an Amherst College folk festival, 1970.

Kerr family gathering in Holywood, County Down, 1956.

May Peirce holds three month old Maggie at McKibbins', 1931.

Maggi and wee cousin Morrell get a wheelbarrow ride from Auntie Vi, c. 1933.

MISS JO JOHNSON FROM THE U.S.A.

We had looked forward for months to the arrival of the friends from America. Mammy would pause, leaning over the sink, the potato peeler motionless in her hand, and her blue eyes filled with "times of long ago." "Tell me about the olden times, Mammy," I used to say, but now she didn't need to be coaxed. One of her girlfriends from childhood was coming home on holiday, from the fabled shores of America.

"They were so much in love," she'd sigh romantically, "I never saw a couple so much in love. He would meet her coming out of the Citadel, the hemstitching company we worked in and it was" — here Mammy would nod at me, bringing me into the story, "as if all Belfast stood still. They'd walk down Bedford Street, heads together and hands clasped." Mammy's voice would trail off and I'd prime her, "so is her husband coming with her?"

Taking up the potato peeler again and gouging out a few eyes from the Kerr Pink, she would confide "Oh no dear, sure he's too busy making thousands." Then she would add, and this was the part I loved best of all, "but her wee daughter's comin' with her. You two will get along like a house on fire, for she's about the same age as you. Her name is Jo-Ann." A hyphenated name — how blissful, I thought. In my class we had names like Joan, Jane, Margaret, Daphne — no nonsense names with hyphens or accents.

At night I would drift off to sleep, thinking of a wonderful new friend from America. She would be as pretty as Shirley Temple and dressed like a Princess. In my mind's eye, I could see her in a cotton dress with panties to match. Panties to match in my eight year old estimation were the bee's knees, the cat's pajamas, the chic to end all chic. I could hardly wait.

On the day of the visit, my sister and I dressed in our best pink matching dresses, smocked across the bodice. Our hair was not only curled, but burnished with Mammy's silk scarf until it shone. Daddy was in his brown suit (his only suit) and his Sunday-go-to-meeting tie. Mammy wore her black wool dress with huge sleeves embroidered in red and white. We shone with cleanliness and a positive bubble of expectancy. Our whole house seemed to hold its breath.

They arrived. The first thing that was a terrible shock to me was that Jo-Ann was plain. No, not plain. Downright ugly. She had sallow skin and two thick plaits of hair that stuck out from each side of her pasty face like your legs on a donkey ride. She was square shaped. Her coat and a hat matched, so far so good. But both hat and coat matched the salmon pink color of her featureless face! I flinched involuntarily. Quickly, though, I remembered my manners. I shook her hand and solemnly piped "Nice to have you with us, Jo-Ann." She was no Shirley Temple.

Twisting up one corner of her mouth she said in a nasal twang "Some small house y'got here," and then to the astonishment of everyone underlined this remark by pulling from her mouth a stream of green bubble gum, which twanged back into place with a little plop. We all jumped slightly.

"Well, yes, yes dear I'm sure it's not what you're used to in America," said Mammy brightly, "but why don't you and Margaret go and play in the hall so that your Mammy and I can get caught up on all our news." Frantically, she ushered the small plump form of her old friend into the comfort of our front room.

Jo-Ann surveyed me. Up and Down. Down and up. I felt my short silk socks with the pink border and my strapped patent leather shoes wither under her scrutiny. Standing in the hallway, our tiled floor glowed in the evening sunlight. The design of rust, green and cream had always pleased me. Kicking the tiles with her high heeled pumps, our visitor curled her lip and said "Don't you have any fitted carpet?" Dumbly, I shook my head. We didn't have any fitted carpet anywhere. "We have fitted carpet all over our house," Jo-Ann said. Then, changing the subject she demanded, "Well, what are we going to do?"

Proudly I took her over to my doll and pram sitting beside my miniscule doll house. Smiling, I asked, "Would you like to play houses? You can be the Mammy and I'll be your wee girl." Her face turned several shades of pink, so quickly I added, "or if you'd rather be the wee girl?"

The door of the sitting room opened and Jo-Ann's mother peeped out, just in time to hear her ewe lamb retort, "What! Play with dolls? Do you think I'm a baby?" Hastily Aunt Ida shoved loose change into her daughter's hands and said, "Now, now, why don't you take Margaret and Dorothy down to the sweetie shop and you can buy some candy."

It was the first time I'd seen Jo-Ann look animated. I rushed into the kitchen where Dorothy was and hissed, "Hey, come on down to Mercer's, Aunt Ida's given ol' whatserface a *pile of money*." Dorothy appeared by our side as if by magic and the three of us trotted down the hill.

Jo-Ann complained, "Ain't you got a car, for gosh sake?"

Dorothy looked at her. She was two years older and three inches taller than our guest. "Uncle Nelson and Uncle Albert do, but we don't," she said with such an air of superiority and finality that the wee Yank was struck dumb.

Mercer's, the sweetie shop, was a small side street shop that sold everything but the kitchen sink. There were rows of hard boiled sweets in glass jars with knobs, at the back of the counter. A leg of ham hung from a hook in the ceiling. Barrels of potatoes, rows of cabbages and turnips met us at the doorway, and in the side windows were shallow boxes full of cheap sweets dear to the hearts of children. "There are flies in the window," sniffed Jo-Ann. "Only two," I answered, wondering what she was moaning about. "Look" I cried, jumping with excitement, "there's jelly babies, licorice, and allsorts." Jo-Ann paid no attention to me. She marched into the dark interior and pounded on the counter. Mr. Mercer, his eyes wide with amazement, shuffled from the back room. "We want marshmallows, Sir" she ordered. Mr. Mercer blinked. "Marsh what?" he said. Stamping her foot Jo-Ann cried "Doggone it, I said marshmallows. Do you Irish know nothing?" Dorothy and I cringed in the doorway. Now what, we thought.

"Young lady," Mr. Mercer said, his voice dropping to a whisper. "Don't let me hear you using language like that in this God-fearing Baptist shop. WE do not have marshmallows. WE have *never* had marshmallows." He waved his arm behind at all the glass jars standing at attention, and lowering his voice even further said "But we have fifty other varieties." He then inspected us. *"Where* is she from?" he asked us.

"I'm from the States, the finest country in the world." Jo-Ann glared at him. "Well young lady, Mr. Mercer replied, "I'd recommend you leave for there as soon as possible, or choose what sweets you want." Becoming aware of the large handful of change she had in her fingers, Mr. Mercer leaned across the counter. "How do you fancy Brazil nut toffee?" Dorothy and I held our breaths. Only at Christmas did anyone buy that.

"Sure, why not?" said our millionaire, pouring the money towards Mr. Mercer. "Give us that much."

"In three separate bags and...? queried the shopkeeper.

"Naw, one. "I'll divide it, replied Jo-Ann." Mr. Mercer winked at Dorothy and me.

Up the street we walked, sucking noisily. We should have not been eating before our meal, but Jo-Ann had stuffed her mouth full of toffee as soon as we'd left the shop, so what else could we do? The toffee was scrumptious.

The tea table was laden by the time we returned to the house. Our best china sparkled against the gleaming white linen damask tablecloth. Sucking her toffee, Jo-Ann refused to eat anything. In the middle of the table there was a large bowl of fruit, kept there more for a centerpiece than anything else.

Jo-Ann took three bananas out of the bowl. As we ate a holiday meal of beef tongue, pork fillet, salad and six kinds of home-baked bread, our visitor stolidly munched her way through the curving cream fruit. As she finished each one, she flung the skins into the centre of the table.

Our mother was magnificent. She did not give any sign of seeing Jo-Ann's despicable table manners. Lovingly, she spoke to her old friend. Happily, she dished out more fillet and tongue. Charmingly, Daddy plied Aunt Ida with another slice of coffee cake, and spoke worriedly about political unrest in Germany. Dorothy and I hardly heard one word of the grown-ups talk. If we had acted at table like Jo-Ann was acting, Daddy would have thundered to us to leave, and Mammy would have rapped our knuckles with the knife handle. Blithely, Jo-Ann ate nothing but the three bananas. In our eyes, she had done the unspeakable. She had refused our hospitality, our fully-laden table.

The rest of the evening passed in embarrassed apologies from Aunt Ida, and bright remarks from Mammy and Daddy about "she must be feeling a bit strange in a foreign land." We were told to take our young visitor for a walk and we did. Jo-Ann looked like a pale tub of salmon pink lard. Neighbors stared at her in the street. We even got a couple of cat-calls coming up Pomona Avenue. "Hey, look at the Yankee lollipop," yelled one of the Kelly boys. Dot and I flung an, "Aw, shut yer face and mind yer own business." But it was just rhetoric, our hearts weren't in it. We thought she looked pretty awful too. Eventually, Aunty Ida and Jo-Ann went home to their relatives.

Our guests were barely out the door, with Mammy and Daddy calling from the front door "Now safe home! You'll have no time to wait for the tram," than our parents came into the cozy sitting room and collapsed in an exhausted heap on the sofa. We all looked at one another and words flew like angry mosquitoes. "What a brat!" "Do you think all Yankee kids are like that?" God forbid! "Poor Ida!" "She lets that kid get away with murder." She was the first foreigner I ever met.

Some six years later and completely out of the blue, a package arrived from Texas. Inside were two long slim boxes addressed to us. Hearts pounding Dorothy and I opened them. Lying on deep velvet were two diamond bracelets and a short note. We could hear Aunt Ida's voice as we read:

> Dear Girls,
>
> I know you'll be surprised to receive these
> as they are really high school graduation
> gifts. My husband and I divorced two years
> ago and Jo-Ann wished to live with him.
> On her graduation we all got together, and
> I presented my daughter with one of these
> Bracelets. It was expensive, but I wanted
> to give her the best.
>
> Jo-Ann would not take it. Said she didn't
> want any part of me. So the next day I
> went out and ordered another one, so
> that you two girls could have one each.
> I hope you enjoy wearing them. I
> would at your age.
>
> Cordially,
> Ida Johnston

And then, in parenthesis…(Aunty)

JOHN KNOX, ODD JOBS MAN

My maternal grandfather, Davy Walker, was a well known "horsey" man. People were drawn from miles around to ask his opinion of a frisky filly or a trotting pony. Reared in Dromore Village, County Down, it was because of the growth of his young family that he and his wife Eva, like many country folk before them, left their green vale to settle in Belfast, the industrial capital of the North of Ireland.

Before long, and to nobody's surprise, he prospered. He not only had a crossroads grocery store at Finaghy, with a gas station opposite and a milk business in Mowen Street next to the Bog Meadows, but he still continued to give advice on horse flesh. He himself even kept a pair of trotters in the livery stable attached to the dairy with its clanking milk urns.

During these years he had casual laborers come and go. One of his most loyal, though somewhat slow-witted, was a man by the name of John Knox. Why anyone ever- gave the poor soul such a name, (for as you well know John Knox was the stern leader of Protestant Reformation in Scotland in the mid-Sixteenth Century), I do not know. Maybe it was some institution's hope that by saddling a foundling with such a name, it might keep him on the straight and narrow. Whatever it was — there was the poor creature branded with a name that was the epitome of solid worth and correctitude. As luck would have it, this unfortunate man ended up, as many a footloose country yokel before him, looking like a ragbag by the time he reached his early sixties.

John had been an odd jobs man for Granda, willing to muck out the stalls or spade up the running sheugh in the courtyard for a pittance of a wage and his seat at the end of a well-laden table. He had neither chick nor child and by the time I met him, he didn't have many teeth either. However, I well remember that day. He arrived at our small suburban house on the outskirts of Strandtown, many long years since Grandfather, whose word was law, had offered a bite at the table to every beggar, old friend or relative fallen on hard times. Nevertheless, such country hospitality dies hard, and my Mother was still set in the old ways. In Belfast they said that if you scratched the skin of any one of us, you would find soil under your nails — meaning that each and every one of us was still only a generation from the ploughed field.

So when John knocked a loud rat-tat on our well polished knocker and asked for my Mother, I ran into the kitchen with a sense of high excitement to tell her "There's a tramp askin' for you at the door Mammy." She peeping out the doorway and scrubbing her hands dry on the roller towel, admonished me with "Augh, it's no such thing child; sure it's John Knox, one of my father's workers. Come on in, John and what are you doin' round this way?"

John, twirling his cap in his hand, shuffled a little and explained, through a mouth spittling with lack of teeth. "Sure, May, you were always the grand girl and I just happened to be in the neighborhood and thought I'd drop in on you and say hello, and maybe have a wee bite and sup." I could see his old eyes wandering toward our scullery where soda farls were cooling on the rack. "Well John," said Mammy "then come on into the kitchen and you can have a cup of tea and then be on your way." My Mother spoke a little sharply, I thought. Instead of sharing the pot of tea, which would have been the usual thing to do with a visitor, she carefully set the table for her unexpected guest alone. I watched.

There he sat, slurping the hot brew from his saucer, spading sugar in, as if five teaspoons to a cup were a normal amount, and spreading the floury-surfaced farls with curling slices of fresh dairy butter. He bit into the bread with all the sharpness that his loose yellow molars could muster.

Having observed this performance with the interested squeamishness of a seven year old, I decided that nothing more could be milked from the experiences and turned to escape to my doll and pram in the garden. By this time, Knox had risen and was following my Mother's slim figure into the dining room, still speaking to her. "Ah now May, weren't you the kindest and best-lookin' of all the Walker girls, and sure didn't I have the quare notion of ye when you were just a slip of a girleen." John giggled happily, and I looked at Mammy thinking how funny all of this seemed, and what a foolish man this John Knox was. With a light laugh and an "Augh, now John, get away with you and all your nonsense," my Mother suddenly called me back. Without any change in the timbre of her voice she said, "Margaret, bring me the mending to do, and get the big scissors out of the ornament on the mantelpiece... there's a pet lamb."

Obediently I went over to Daddy's chair and shakily poised myself on the arm in order to reach the ornament above. Carefully, I fished the pair of scissors from its innards and jumped to the floor, reaching them to my Mother.

John Knox, still smelling slightly of stable, floury soda bread and a sour odor which I did not recognize, but was mixed up with sawdust on wet floors and swinging doors on a Friday night down at the Arches, stood swaying slightly in the late afternoon sunlight. My Mother and he stood as if jelled in a yellow sunbeam. It was so quiet I could see dust motes dancing in the air. She stood, with her short frizzed hair licking around her ears, one roughened hand gripping the chair back, one foot awkwardly locked round the ankle of the other. With the thumb of her other hand she slowly flicked the sharp point of the shears. Her visitor, ugly red veins running in profusion through the stubbly growth of beard on his cheeks, stood opposite to her, blinking and continuing to murmur about the good old days when Mr. Walker was alive. Finally these phrases petered out to a few incoherent niceties. Patting me on the head, he finally ambled out the front door, thanking us for the tea.

We never saw John Knox again. Years later I realized that he was typical of the poor country simpleton, uneducated, untrained, who had left whatever hedgerow he had grown up under to try to make a living in the big town. It was not his way of life; the city people with their hurry and scurry were not his kind of people. The second generation of country folk was climbing the social ladder by that time and had joined the industrial squalor of a ship building city. He was a lost soul, and like many a lost soul before him, he had knocked about from one job to another, comforting himself by way of cheap gin and by returning every now and again to one or another of the Walker family, who had known him when he was a younger man.

"But why Mam," I asked a score of years later "did you bring him in when you'd only known him as a girl, and why did you ask me to get you the scissors?" Mammy, who by that time was a white-haired widow, pushed her glasses firmly up her large nose and replied "Because he was of the old days, and you never refuse kith or kin a bite and a sup. But then, when I became aware that he'd been drinking," here her voice dropped to a whisper of outrage, "that's why I asked for the scissors. After all, there were only the two of us in the house, and if he had made a grab at either of us, well...."

Slowly, I turned on my Mother. "You mean to say you would have stabbed him?"

Matter-of-factly Mammy answered, "Oh yes dear, as soon as I heard him talkin' a lot of old nonsense and the worse for drink, I made up my mind. Of course, thank God, I never needed to do anything. But if I had had to, I was ready. I always keep my scissors sharp you know, I didn't work in a hemstitching company for nothing!" Quietly, she tucked her latest pair of scissors into her workbasket and went singing into the scullery, and it was only then that I understood how mothers are the bravest and most foolhardy people in the whole wide world.

BOOKWORMS

From the day I read "The Cat Sat on the Mat" — the very first sentence I ever tried to learn and realized I could not only decipher the letters but noted that three of the words all sounded the same, I was off and running. No book was too deep for me, no magazine too light. I read comic-cuts when I was five and the *Girls Chrystal,* a tony magazine for girls when I was twelve, and nobody ever tried to improve my reading or scold me for reading tripe. You see, my Mother never read, being too busy polishing furniture and seeing that all the blinds hung at the right height in our windows. Daddy usually fell asleep over his book from the library, tired out after points duty — traffic cop duty — at rush hour at the Arches.

My sister Dot encouraged me and being four years older threw Russian tomes, Dickens and Jane Austin my way, long before I was ready for them. But did this quench my fervor for books? Chomp! Chomp! I went, and they lay at my young feet — conquered stacks of literature.

Suddenly, by the time I was nine, our Mother woke up to the fact that she had bookworms for daughters. She would wring her hands and wail to her sisters (she had a surfeit of those), "My God Aileen, or Evie, or Vi...," or whoever. "No man will be interested in them. They're going to be intelligent and *show* it." This, in Belfast life was a real no-no. If you were intelligent, you had to smother it under girlish giggles and a taste for high fashion or cookery classes. No male must ever learn that you had grey matter worthy of attention, until you had him safely down the church aisle. Once so, then *Bang!* You could wallop him with your brilliance. The Aunts tut-tutted in sympathy. They all had sons. We sucked the tail-ends of our hair ribbons and continued to read, regardless of all the hysteria, curled up in quiet hideaways in our well polished home.

But something happened that changed our Mother's viewpoint, and it started with dislike. There was a neighbor nearby who had been a teacher, was English-born, wore spectacles behind which gleamed two sparkling dark intelligent eyes, and had a large family. They had the same surname as we had but whereas our father was a beat-walking policeman, their father was a banker and prosperous. Our Mammy had to save for two years to buy one winter coat. Her namesake had a new jacket every summer and a new long coat every Easter and Christmas. Mammy, although she never admitted it, was green with envy.

We liked Mrs. Kerr and would wave at her as we strolled by, noses stuck in our latest library book. She would ask us what we were reading and would nod approval as we replied, "Henty, L.M. Montgomery, Ballentine, Thackeray."

One day she stopped the three of us as we hurried along the avenue to catch the tram. Mammy was immediately on her guard. I sensed this by the nervous cough she gave. "My, you do look nice! Going into town?" Turning to us Mrs. Kerr asked, "Funny to see you pair without your usual book." We laughed, taking this for a joke.

Mammy, immediately on the defensive said, "Indeed I've reared a couple of old bookworms; it's all they're good for". We examined the toes of our shoes. Here we go again, I thought.

There was a pause.

"You must never say that, Mrs. Kerr," our neighbor said. "You are lucky to have children fond of reading, for there is no learning like it." Mammy gave a tight little smile and said that we must hurry. As soon as we were out of earshot, she exclaimed, "Who does she think she is, telling me what I can or cannot say about my girls. The cheek of her!" We said nothing. "Did you hear her?" Mammy questioned Dot, "Do you not think she should mind her own business?"

My sister, even at fifteen, was wise beyond her years. She and Mammy quarreled all the time, yet it was to Dot that Mammy would turn for advice or opinion and not me. Dot linked her arm through Mammy's and then said, "Mammy, I went to school with all her sons and daughters. They're all bright, but there's not a real reader among them. It must have been an awful disappointment to her."

Mammy licked her lips, which she always did when she was bewildered. "Do you mean she's jealous of me, for having two daughters who read?" Dot shook her head, "No Mammy, not jealous, I think envious might be the better word".

From that day forward when someone remarked on our love of books, Mammy would slyly say, "I've a couple of bookworms, and only the Lord knows where it will take them." More than complacent, for once, Mammy sounded genuinely pleased with herself.

MEIN HUT ER HAT DREI ECKEN

It is the only title this story could actually have. A silly German song, one of those rollicking, interminable jolly rounds that we all used to boom out in our misspent youth in Jugendherberges, in the Swiss Alps. As soon as I heard the rhyme:

> *My hat it has three corners*
> *Three corners has my hat*
> *And if it has not three corners*
> *Then that is not my hat*

I thought of Easter and Tyrella and the year I made a three cornered highwayman's hat. It was not an easy task, but Mammy had said I could do whatever I wanted with my long outgrown headgear in pale pink tweed with the velvet trim.

Our family, and by that I mean not our small unit family but the *real* family, i.e. two uncles, three aunts, Mammy and the five of us — Morrell, Derek, Jack, Dot and I — always went to County Down for Easter. We had been doing so from time immemorial. We visited the McKibbins, a typical farming family, two spinsters and a bachelor brother, in their 18th Century farmhouse.

While the grownups sat and chatted in the kitchen, we children raced to the long meadow and trundled our colored Easter eggs down the hill until they broke. Then we ate them dipped in coarse salt filched from the old fashioned saltbox. After this traditional pastime we were free to scramble through overgrown gardens, climb stone dykes, push the millstone at the back of the barn round its axis and play whatever game Morrell and Dot had thought up for us that year. In March, Dot had confided in me that this Easter the game would be "coaches and highwaymen." This meant cutting out and sewing a proper highwayman hat, a finger-pricking and careful cutting job. Just before the big day, I had finally completed it. I had kept my hat a secret and couldn't wait to see how surprised Dot would be when she saw my wonderful creation.

All of our games were, of course, "pretend." Our horses were visualized by whacking our rumps and whinnying; our Indians were crowned by turkey feathers; our guns for shooting one another stone dead were sticks from the hedgerows. (When you died you had to roll on the ground feigning mortal agony.) But this year I had a *real* hat! The color — a washed-out pink — was a bit strange for a highwayman. But the shape was just perfect.

It was the year after war declaration, 1940. For us, Easter at the McKibbins was all that it was expected to be. The journey down by bus was bumpy, every time we went under a bridge we all cheered. Bertie, the bus driver, greeted yearly like a long lost Uncle, was as funny as ever. The world sailed by us in a happy haze of new woolly lambs and yellow primroses dotting the banks on each side of the country road. As usual the McKibbins were welcoming. We scampered up the big open field, rolled our hard boiled eggs in their purple, green and yellow glory (plus some with little faces of Hitler, which we smashed gleefully).

After a proper holiday dinner, we children ran off to play. When no one was looking, I slipped on my three cornered hat as my turn was called. "All right, Margaret, it's your time to be the highwayman, now hide behind the bushes," Dot ordered. I clattered out with Mammy's black scarf over the lower part of my face and shouted, "Halt! Your money or your *life*," feeling so pleased with myself for really looking the part.

There was a stunned silence. "Give me that hat," Dot said. "It's my turn now."

"No, it's mine! I made it, only I'm wearing it," I shouted, and slapping my thigh I crashed through the gateway and galloped down the lane on my imaginary steed.

"It's a silly game anyway," Dot yelled after me, "who needs to be a silly highwayman?"

I stopped. My big sister had always been our leader. Morrell, Derek and Jack slowed their pursuit after my pink three cornered hat and shuffled their feet. "Yay, I'm tired," agreed Morrel, our second in command. Jack and Derek ran over to the hedge to look at the new lambs in the corner field. I turned, my horse forgotten, my mask slipping….I wanted Dot so much to continue with our wonderful game. I tore the strap from under my chin and held the hat out to her.

"Dot, Dot," I cried. "I didn't mean it. Take it. Wear it — please." My sister, my dear big sister of the fair hair and the serious face frowned a little. "No" she said. I suppose I'm really getting too old to play these sorts of games." With that, she wheeled round and marched in to the grownups.

I stood in the sweet scented garden, with the fat bumble-bees clambering drunkenly from fuchsia lantern to fuchsia lantern and felt my heart breaking. Dorothy was leaving me, and it was *all my fault*. No longer would she be our fearless leader, no more would she make up our marvelous games.

If only I had kept my mouth shut, if only I hadn't been filled with pride about my hat, Dot would have continued playing with us. She would have looked so daring — truly like a real highwayman — in my three cornered hat. Her swashbuckling bravado would easily have outshone my own. I would have held my sister back for another year in our world of innocent certainty, where willow wands were whips, a stone was a magic talisman, and our little world, guarded so carefully by Dot and Morrell, would remain steady and safe by the power of their imagination.

Or did it not happen that way at all? Did Dot see her small malleable sister disagree with her for the first time, refusing to give up to her, the elder, what she desired? I'll never know for certain, because Dot swears she doesn't recall any of this, but I remember the headiness of first opposing my idol, and then wanting, so desperately, to return to my place in the familiar hierarchy. But that Easter the die was cast and there was no turning back.

A LITTLE CHINA FIGURE

In every working class home in Belfast there is found, invariably, something dear to the mother's heart — beside her children of course. I mean an object, maybe something inherited, such as a clock, a bowl, a lovely ornament, or maybe just something she fancies.

In the early years of my childhood, my Mother had inherited little. But at the beginning of her marriage she had bought, with her own money — and mind you it was difficult to save in those days — a china figure of a lady in an Arabic costume. It was shortly after the opening in Egypt of the tomb of Tutankhamen and everything eastern was the rage. That small china figure seemed to hold court, lording it over our sitting room.

She wore a turban made of silky cloth, a burnt gold in color to match the little dhoti which encircled her slim hips and didn't quite cover one raised leg. Her pose was somewhat like "The Thinker" in the hallway of the main Belfast Public Library. But instead of a hairy old man, she was elegance personified.

The turban was held in place by a shiny red button and underneath a small fuzz of black hair peeped from either side of her face. And what a face! Her cheeks were slightly flushed, her eyes almond-shaped with two lines underneath for emphasis. Her mouth was a perfect bow. We always called her "Mammy's lady" and she sat on our rosewood table in the sitting room. She was not really china, but some kind of bisque and we adored her almost as much as Mammy did.

One afternoon our cousin Tom and his pal dropped in to visit. They lived in Holywood, some four miles away, so their arrival was rather a surprise. After scoffing some of Mammy's soda bread and cake, they got ready to depart. Then for some reason Tom pulled the cap off his friend's head and off they went tearing and yelling through the house.

Before they had even reached the sitting room, Dot and I knew, instinctively, what was about to happen. By the time we reached the doorway, they were circling round the small table. As Ronny grabbed Tom's cap, the table tilted and down fell Mammy's lady, shattering into a million pieces.

It was a traumatic event in our young lives. The war was on at that time, but nothing horrified us half as much as those china slivers on our maroon carpet. We never forgot that random accident. I never forgave Tom for it. Perhaps if he had been a cousin from Mammy's side of the family it might have been easier to forgive, but he was from the paternal side, the Kerrs. That made all the difference. It may sound unkind, but in Ireland the maternal side is always stronger.

At least fifty years passed. Dot and I had grown up, traveled, and married "foreigners." But like all Irish today, we always went home on visits. One afternoon we decided to walk over the hills to Holywood where Tom and his wife lived in retirement. Cousin Tom had been an Architect. Now he had returned to his first love, for which he is renowned. He is a water-colorist. That day he threw open the door in welcome saying, "I wondered who the two oul' dolls were on the doorstop!" We roared with laughter and told him he'd better watch out or we'd give him a clip on the ear. It is always good to see a cousin, and over the intervening years we had grown to know and love many of our Kerr cousins.

Naturally, we talked of days gone by. Suddenly Tom said "Gawd, we loved goin' up to Aunty May's. Ye know, after our Mammy died we never saw a sweet thing come into our house. Your Mammy was a great baker." We nodded in fond agreement, and then Tom leaned forward and confided, "You know, I never got over breaking yon wee lady in the front room. Only God knows why we ran in there. I'll never forget Aunty May's face." He shook his head, and looked at the floor.

"Ah, never mind Tom." Dot said, "Worse things have happened in this world since." Talk drifted to other matters.

On the walk home, while the midges rose from damp hedges in waves and the lights of Belfast city sprang below us, I said to Dot, "I'm glad that Tom apologized to us. I never knew that he realized what he'd done."

"Aye," said Dot, "and I never realized that he and his pal walked all that way to our house for Mammy's baking because Aunt Lena had died. They were left so young without a mother — but of course we didn't understand". "Right!" I answered, "and we took everything for granted: Mammy, her wee buns and her soda bread. Us having her, we didn't realize either."

Maturity and forgiveness come slow to the Irish.

BUNNY

It was lying in a ditch sloshing with stagnant water. We saw movement on the brackish surface. Derek, then six, fished it out, a frightened rabbit covered in slime and wet weeds.

The rabbit lay, jerking, in Derek's open hands while we gathered round. Dot was fourteen then so we wheeled on her to hear what she'd say. "The poor wee thing, it's soaking wet," Dot held out her skirt.

We dried the tiny animal as best we could. My cousin Morrell, my age — but years older in knowledge, shook his head. "It's not goin' to last." He looked at us. "There's somethin' wrong with it."

"Augh, maybe it's just hungry," I said. I was always thinking of food and felt that all our patient needed was a good sup of milk. We bore it home. Our Mothers, sympathizing with us God love them, gave us a white rag soaked in milk to see if it might lip some. Auntie Aileen surveyed it and confirmed Morrell's dark assessment. "It's jerkin' somethin' awful." By then we had lapped it in old toweling. It looked like a wee furry baby.

The rabbit had ears like seashells. It was so young, they weren't even very long. Underneath a tender, wiggling pink nose, we could see perfect sharp teeth. "Look at its whiskers," Dot breathed. We gazed down with a kind of reverence that only children reared in kindness themselves could feel. We had never examined a wild baby creature before, at such close quarters.

"Can we keep it Mammy and make it a pet?" I begged. Mammy shook her head. "Darlin,' she warned, "You can count on nothing in this life. Thon poor wee animal doesn't look right to me." I stared down. I so wanted it to be well. I wished it would drink the milk, but all it did was spit instead of suck and the jolting jarring movement of its body had not ceased.

"I'm sure it's getting better," Derek insisted. Although I was three years older, I quickly saw that we shared an urgent hope for our little found friend. We both wanted it to live with every fiber of our young beings.

"We'll ask Uncle Albert when he arrives," Dot decided. Because she was boss of our child circle, we all agreed and ran down the lane toward the road, carrying our little bundle.

"What's 'ya got there?" yelled some of the country boys from school. Resolutely we turned away from them. We were from the city, evacuees from the German bombing, set down in the strange and marvelous countryside of Killinchy. We loved the place, but felt strangers with the "country yins." We mistrusted their cruel ways. Luckily the boys didn't come after us as we — thankfully — made for the bus stop further down the road.

We had some ten minutes to wait for the bus and during this time we poured over our find. "I saw it first," Derek said, stroking between the rabbit's ears. "I wiped off all his mud," I interrupted. "Shut up!" Morrell said gruffly. Dot bit her lip. "Let's hear what Uncle Albert says." Derek and I stroked the bunny, murmuring. "There there wee pet, we'll fix you." The tiny animal kept up its fevered movement.

Here's Daddy now," Morrell shouted as the bus hove into sight. A tall, military figure with a neat moustache alighted and was engulfed in bear hugs from our cousins. Dot and I hung back. I held the basket.

"What have we here?" Our Uncle bent over the basket as the boys explained all that had happened. "Let's see the poor thing." Our Uncle held the small beast in his hand, examined it and with one swift, clean gesture, wrung the bunny's neck. His large carpenter's hands moved with such sureness, and then deftly tucked the limp body into its wrappings. "Nothing could have been done," he said, "Its back was broken."

The four of us stood and wept. Bunny was dead, but the worry and illness that we could neither comprehend nor cope with was also ended. We were filled with relief, even while our tears continued to splash.

"Let's give him a prince's burial," exclaimed Dot, the bookworm. "In a reed bed," I promised, though my voice was cracking. "With berries all around him like a wreath," said Derek, his eyes still shining with tears. "I'll dig the hole," Morrell offered. Off we scampered to the funeral.

I turned round to wave at Uncle Albert who was walking slowly down the lane. As a policeman in the ruined, blitzed city of Belfast, he must have seen pain, loss and fire. Here in the safe and verdant fields of County Down, his young family had had a foretaste of death. I can still see his smile as he returned my salute.

Of course at that time I did not know his thoughts. Mulling it over years and years later, I know that nobody can be shut off from death, no matter how kindly parents and governments try to fend off the Grim Reaper from those they would protect.

Uncle Albert was the mercy killer on that day. Momentarily shocked, in the end we had not been disappointed. He had known what to do and carried it out. Of such actions are heroes made. Ours had a neat moustache.

THE SECRET PLACE

We each have one, even to this day. I have a barn-red bench in the back garden where I skulk with a book on days when people and worries encroach. On those days, I just read, to stare into space, think my own thoughts.

Other people have them too. In everyone's life there is a certain secret place that answers some need hidden deep within. I have heard of little boys sitting in closets sucking their thumbs contentedly for half an hour. One elderly man I know loved to stand down by the sea, near a breakwater. He said the sound of the waves allowed him to "ruminate." *There's a word* you don't hear too often in this harried world.

When my cousins and I were children, we lived in a city of tidy back gardens and whitewashed yards. But when war came, we were evacuated to Killinchy, County Down, where we faced grand open spaces of green fields and woodlands, rivers that curled through meadows and rivers that overflowed. These spaces were new to us, awesome and foreign. Derek, Dot, Morrell and I wandered in all of this immensity of nature, delighted and somewhat overcome by the size of it all. We were struck by the absence of houses with neat railings and shut gates to keep us in order.

After a few months Derek, three years younger than me, and I began to long for a small, tidy place reminiscent of our home in the red-bricked city. While trotting through an overgrown wood, near to the Blackwater, we turned a corner and there it was — a low cave of green made by laurel bushes growing in profusion. At the center was a hole where we could crouch and creep in. It was just the right size for two lost city cousins.

The space was oval shaped, and although hidden, light glimmered through the leaves making the room like an enchanted chamber. We hunkered down and discussed what we should do with it. Over the next few weeks we brushed the floor with willow wands, brought in two small logs to sit on, and a broken blue china rabbit that we'd found in a ditch. Placing him up on an inner branch, we had a little house! Every day after school we would sit on our respective logs and discuss our teachers. Derek found stones to decorate the entry way and I brought in flowers I'd picked in the hedgerows. Nobody knew about it except Derek and me.

But of course, eventually we had to show it to someone. My sister and Derek's brother Morrell smiled kindly at us and said "it was nice." What need had driven us to show it to an outsider? Was it the desire that springs unbidden to have what we have made admired by those who are *not* related? I will never know, but finally we brought Dorothy Heron, an older, quite sophisticated ten year old from school. She said that she'd like to see our secret place. Thrilled with her effusive show of interest, we bore her along through the woods and then shyly stood at the portal of our forest home saying, "Look! Here it is."

She bent down, crawled though the entry, and stood up in the wonderful green chamber. Dust motes danced in the air; sunbeams mottled the undersides of leaves and branches. A smile curled her lip and laughter spluttered from her. "This," she said, "A secret place? It's silly!" Turning, she flicked our blue china bunny to the ground and swinging her school satchel to her shoulder she brushed past Derek's rocks, knocking them every which way. "Young kids, that's what you are."

The magic disappeared. I don't think Derek or I ever went back to our private place. An outsider had sneered at it and criticized it. Therefore we, too, turned our backs to it.

Yet last year Derek, now a man in his sixties, suddenly said "D'ye mind that wee place we had in the woods in Killinchy? Do you remember trying to plant green corn?"

"So we did," I said. "I'd quite forgotten, the corn I mean, not the place. I never forgot that."

"Me neither," said Derek, and we smiled at one another, the way loving cousins do, who once shared childhood and a secret spot of sun motes and green.

"What did you call that girl who spoilt it all?" he asked.

"The right wee bitch, she was." We grinned at one another. We hadn't known that word then, but it was good to use it fifty years later.

CAPTAIN HARRIS

It all began easily enough. At the age of twelve, I was a lumpy girl at Strandtown Public Elementary School and no doubt more serious that I should have been. Mr. Martin, our Principal, called me out of class one day. I had been chosen to baby-sit three year old Brian Harris, the only child of Captain and Mrs. Harris. I was to ask my mother's permission and report to him the next day.

In Belfast where I was reared, work by any young person was frowned upon. In my mother's working class book only the poverty-stricken could sell newspapers at street corners or run messages for a penny. However, when I was passing on the request that evening I also mentioned that Captain Harris was in the military and English. This was during World War II and somehow as the English in Ireland were "strangers in a strange land" — and with him being a Captain no less — the winds of change swept in a different direction. Hence I found myself earning the princely sum of half a crown for every evening spent in the Harris's sparsely but so differently furnished home in Belmont.

Up until that time I had rarely been in strangers' houses. To that point, I had been ensconced in two huge clans of my own family, where kitchen ranges, knitted cushion covers, dark oak sideboards and many-runged chairs expressed normality and order. At the Harris's, I discovered light Swedish furniture with stick legs. There was space everywhere and books in low stretching bookcases taking up half a wall. It was the books that appealed to me. Brian, their fair-haired little boy with rosy cheeks, tiny white teeth and blue eyes — so different from our pale skinned, dark haired look — was a sweet child and no bother. His mother was lovely, soft spoken and charming. Captain Harris, though handsome, was somewhat aloof.

Time passed. I started real work at the age of fourteen so baby-sitting ended and life for me began. My sister and I went youth hostelling every weekend, scrambling though bog and heather, climbing mountains and beginning to cast our eyes toward Scotland or the continent for holidays. The war was over and a sense of adventure permeated our plans. We shouldered our rucksacks and started off to unknown places, both within Ireland and beyond.

I must have been about seventeen. The London railway station was filled with smoke, steam and noise. Dot and I alighted from the train, Dot in front as we hurried along the platform. Rushing to keep up with her, I suddenly spied Captain Harris and Brian standing together, looking up the railway track. I walked up to them and said "Hello Captain Harris, how are you. Do you remember me? I'm Margaret Kerr. I used to baby sit Brian." Captain Harris looked right through me. I felt hurt and nonplussed and, bending down, as best I could with my heavy rucksack on my back, I said, "Hello Brian, don't you remember me?" but he too pretended not to see me.

I was stunned. I hurriedly took to my heels and fled after Dot. Catching up with her, I said, "Did you see me talking to Captain Harris and the wee boy? I can't get over it. Bloody English, wouldn't even say Hello to me now, no wonder people say the English are stuck up." I was fuming.

"Oh, never mind," said Dot, "let's put a step on it, or we'll never catch our connection to Dover." Off we went to France.

Years passed. My sister had lived in America but returned to Edinburgh, Scotland where I was then working. One Saturday morning, the day stretching in front of us, we were talking over the littered breakfast table. I had just put down my teacup when suddenly, for no reason whatsoever, I looked at Dot and asked, "Do you remember that time on the London railway platform when Captain Harris and young Brian refused to speak to me?"

Dot looked up from her newspaper. "Yes dear, sort of vaguely, I remember you yammering on about it and called him snooty English or something. Why? It was an awfully long time ago."

I looked across the table feeling almost foolish for what I was going to say. I said, 'Dot, something, I realize now, was odd. Captain Harris was still in full wartime uniform and Brian…" I stopped here, my breath shallow. "Brian was still the same little boy I had baby-sat. When I saw him that day at least four years had passed since the war was well and truly over."

That Christmas I flew home to be with my people and quite by chance I bumped into my old school principal Mr. Martin as we was striding, maybe not quite as forcefully as once, along North Road. We chatted affably. He was pleased to hear how I loved Edinburgh and then, carelessly, I threw into the conversation "Whatever happened to Captain Harris? Remember, I sat for their son Brian for two years?" Mr. Martin's shaggy eyebrows rose. "But I thought you would have heard Margaret," he said. "It was a terrible tragedy. His wife had been visiting her parents somewhere in the midlands and the Captain and his son went to the London train to meet her. The station took a direct hit. Sorry I can't remember which one." He smiled ruefully and added "The mind isn't as keen as it once was."

But I knew, and to this day I can still see those two figures, one tall in khaki, one little, waiting for the train from the north.

THE AWAKENING

When I was fourteen, I was taller than any of my classmates. Feeling out of place in school, I wanted to start working in the adult world. The sooner the better. A mere six months had passed between Public Elementary School and Business School, before I found myself, a broth of a girl in nylon stockings and purple lipstick, working in the wage office of a small Hemstitching Company off Ormeau Avenue in the centre of Belfast. My duties were simple enough and the office cheerful, being a portioned off corner of the workroom, where the window, reminiscent of the studio in *La Boheme,* reached up to the ceiling, flooding light on the pressers in the workroom side and Mr. Maxwell and me on the other.

There were some forty women and girls in the big stitching room, and it took me no time at all to gather that there was a hierarchy as rigid and plutocratic as the Court of Louis XIV... and a good deal scarier to boot. For example, the embroiderers kept their distance from the stitchers, whose work was sewing up bibs and small linens. They were polite but distant. The examiners, who studied with care every stitch of linen that passed out the door in long white boxes, felt they were better than either stitchers or embroiderers. Prone not only to airs of superiority, but to a "put-on" accent which had to be heard to be believed, examiners felt they were the royalty of the lot. Instead of "I" they say "Ay" and instead of "wumman" (for the female sex) they said "woe-man." Sometimes their polite accent and the ancient grammar would clash profoundly, and I'd overhear such remarks as "Ay was jus' sayin' to thon wee woe-man across wer street." Their carrying-on made me suddenly aware that grammatical gaffes are more difficult to shrug off than an accent, and it was better to have no mode of speech other than your own.

In a class to themselves for humor, hard work and bluntness (noted for calling a spade a bloody shovel) were the smoothers. There were four of them. They stood in front of the big window, daily ironing whatever was put in front of them to a gleaming, almost mirror-like sheen. The only irons they used were noisy, sputtering, gas- popping ones which cleaved the rough cloth like a tramp steamer parting Atlantic waves. Therefore the smoothers would argue, yell, abuse and laugh uproariously, knowing full well they could not be heard above the sound of their irons and the sewing machines. The exception of course was the "Ay" group in the nearby corner and Clarissa, the Forewoman.

It was this group of smoothers I grew fond of. Whenever my clerking job became boring, I would quickly nip round the corner to the ironing table and there I would learn all sorts of tips. For example, you must always smooth handkerchiefs crosswise, and pure linen must be truly damp for perfect work. They could chant such hints like a litany. For all the weight of their aged irons, they would not deign to use new-fangled electric ones. Their women wisdom and earthiness of speech I found wonderfully attractive and I listened carefully to whatever came up in conversation. Unfortunately, my education grew by leaps and bounds. Had my Mother known of the variety of topics discussed, her hair would have curled itself!

Rita, the saucy one, who wore tight-fitting slacks when skirts and dresses were the order of the day, was heard to announce "He just loves washing me in a basin; brings it into the fireside, and dries me all over." As I was in earshot, all the more interesting details were firmly snuffed out by a volley of ssshshhhhs from the other three. A week later I came in to inform Rita that her husband was at the door, wanting to speak to her. She had no sooner departed than Mary took a skelly down the corridor and returned to inform us "That's not her hubby. Yon's her fancy man." Instantly my nubile fourteen year old mind summed up that the cauliflower-eared gentleman in the drafty hallway was the one who liked Rita in a basin. Never having been my fortune, my face — open as a book — revealed my thoughts. At that, the other women crowed with delight. "Aye, that's him. Can y'imagine, in a basin?" Off we all went, shrieking like banshees. Clarissa, the forewoman if you remember, glared at us all for being happy at our work.

Some days they discussed how often you should have sex at night. Old Mrs. O'Donnell, who was one of the few Catholics in the building (but-never-mind; she-is-one-of-the-best), said that he was her husband and she refused him nothing. The other women looked at her pityingly, whereas I thought her as being very romantic. As she was as broad as she was long and had swollen ankles, it was a wee bit difficult to stretch the imagination. Mary admitted that if she were tired she just said "Aw, give us a bit of a rest; I've been on m'feet all day." Then Jinny guffawed, "Aye, but surely you do that on yer back!" Off we all went, screaming again.

The two "Ay" group women were not too sure they approved of young Miss Kerr standing around listening to "coorse" conversation, so for a while I was kept in the office. But there was simply not enough to keep me busy at my desk. Besides, the boss had a penchant for pretty stitchers and would have them in to talk to him about their worries. He certainly did not want a big, lanky lassie like me spoiling his role of the sympathetic ear, so out I would go again.

One of the afore-mentioned pretty stitchers would sometimes disappear for an afternoon. It turned out she was traipsing off to the movies with my Boss. Although an old married woman of five years, she could toss her flowing hair like a seventeen year old. "Just so long as he makes up my piece work," she would say. "Make sure you tell him that," and I would be left at my desk every Friday mumbling "Oh Mr. Maxwell, Annie Connelly was in and said that the Wednesday she was out, that you had to make it up to her." Sure enough, when Clarissa would come in on pay night Mr. Maxwell, with an air of superior indifference, would add to his usual orders "Oh, by the way Clarissa, mind and make Annie's pay up to the usual amount. She was on a message for me last Wednesday." The forewoman and I would look at one another, both knowing what the "message" was. But Loyalty was Clarissa's watchword, and she kept saying Mr. Maxwell was as pure as the driven snow. The smoothers would all chorus, "But he drifted…" and then would collapse over their table, laughing till the tears flowed.

I didn't join in against my Boss, as he was always decent to me. I knew what side my bread was buttered on and always pretended not to hear that he liked women with big busts. However, having a look at Annie's the next day, I had to agree that you surely knew she was coming before she turned the corner. This was kind of interesting to me as bodies, or parts thereof, were never mentioned in our house. If a girl had shapely legs, my Mother described them as "lovely limbs" which though certainly alliterative, puts you off the scent.

Besides Mr. Maxwell, we did have another man in the Company. We had two more, as a matter of fact, but one was just a constant visitor. Wee Jimmie was next door to being a cripple. He was hunch-backed and had a wall eye, but this didn't stop him from keeping the tea room tidy, and the fag-ends swept up round the gas fire. Every evening he would clear up the threads and cuttings with old wet tea leaves. It was from him that I learned to use spent tea leaves to clean up a messy floor.

He was a kindly soul, but his head, being cocked to the side, called forth all kind of remarks from the stitchers. "Trying to look at my legs, Jimmie?" they would call. "I was doin' no such thing! I've better things to do with m'time," he would retort. "Is that so Jimmie. You must tell us about them; did you see under her skirts last night? And if you did, did you know what to do?" The girls gave him an endlessly hard time. Instead of being flustered or embarrassed, Jimmie seemed to get enjoyment out of their ribbing. He was capable of giving back better than he got: "She was a helluva better lookin' than yous ones an' better manners any day," he'd chuckle, happily knocking the tea leaves from the yellow teapot and brushing round the remainders of the day's lunches.

I asked Mary once if Jimmie really did have a girlfriend. "Augh, God no, of course not, what woman in her right mind would look at that poor cratur! But sure he loves the coddin,' and it does no harm." Then she added, "Talk's cheap."

The other man was old Charlie from Jones Sewing Machine Shop, who could fix an awkward or temperamental machine better than anyone. However, when I telephoned for him, there would invariably be a long silence at the other end of the phone. "Ah, well now Miss Kerr, would Sammy the young one not do as well?" Then there would be a little laugh, "You see, Charlie is indisposed today." Before long I understood that Charlie drank like a fish, occasionally had the DTs and had not only a foul temper but an even fouler mouth. When he eventually wandered in the door, a toolbox under his arm, he not only repaired the machine until it purred happily, but he then informed the user what stupid, despicable actions had led to the breaking down of the bobbin, belt, needle, etc. I grew used to mopping up the tears of elderly embroiderers, whose ears, they swore, had never heard such language as Charlie used. I never pointed out to them that neither had I. It was interesting, uncouth, nearly incomprehensible speech to my teen ears. Once, I asked the smoothers what a certain word meant that I heard Charlie mutter as he reached the stairwell, and watched them, as a body, fall in a paroxysm of laughter. I thereafter buttoned my lips carefully and endeavored to banish the mechanic's vocabulary from my thoughts (if not my memory).

Shortly before I left the Hemstitching Company one of the nicest stitchers, Minnie, got engaged. On the day she left there was a huge parade of all the young girls in the place, carrying a huge chamber-pot filled to the brim with salt. On top of the salt sat a celluloid baby doll. They trooped into the workroom singing the usual Belfast wedding song:

> *Here comes the bride*
> *Sixty inches wide*
> *See how she wobbles*
> *Her big backside*

They presented Minnie with the pot. Blushing with happiness at this good luck symbol, forgetting all the cross words and petty arguments of the past, remembering only the happy times of work well done and singing while the machines whirred, Minnie smilingly accepted the gift.

I watched her as she returned to her machine, cleaning it in readiness for some other operator on the following Monday. She oiled and cleaned it, swept up every crumb or dusty corner and went outside to throw out the panful. Returning, she found a boot box at her workplace. Immediately the whole room grew still. I stood near Clarissa, having just brought in the wage packets for that day. The indrawn breath and tut-tuts of some of the older women were heavy upon my ears.

"Open it, open it" the women cried. "No, no, I'll take it home," Minnie replied, trying to bundle it away in her string bag. "Ye won't, ye won't," called out the women. Mr. Maxwell and Jimmie disappeared like lightning. Hesitantly, Minnie began to open the box. Annie Connelly crept up behind her and jolted her elbow so that the contents were open to view.

"Shame, shame" some of the older women admonished. In the box lay an 18" cloth penis, well sewn and stuffed to bursting. I asked "What is it? What is it?" "Augh, nothin' dear, just bride stuff," I was told. I could feel my face growing hot. I was not too sure of what I had seen, but wishing to appear casual and grown-up, I asked "Who made it?" "The gypsy," "The tinker," came from every quarter. Quietly, I walked from the room....

This was my first brush with sexuality, not counting dirty diagrams on school lavatory walls. I told no one. Even my friends, the smoothers, did not mention the incident, except remarking "That gypsy carried things a bit too far." To this day I do not know if this "gift" was typical of the linen houses of the

1940s or whether the half-starved looking woman with poor teeth had brought the custom from a Romany background.

I do know that, in looking back to this youthful period, there was both horror and enticement in the male symbol, both fear and attraction toward a world about which I knew nothing. All around me adult life was drawing me into its sensual, sexual coils, not only with the culmination of Minnie's last day, but in the titillating discussions of the smoothers, the joking of wee Jimmie, the unknown sexual vocabulary of Charlie the drunken mechanic, and Mr. Maxwell's desires.

Retracing my thoughts and feelings of that time, I realize that part of me tingled with the excitement of the physical unknown. But the other part of me, the clear-headed, analytical me, drew back, recoiling from unknown territory, and returned me with deep relief to adventure books and safe daydreams of knights in shining armor.

DANCING AT MAXIM'S

To start off, you had to be approved for membership, which, in itself, leant an aura of sophistication to the dancehall in the centre of Belfast. There was the name, too, *Maxim's*, smacking of flighty high society we may have read about but never seen, except in grey dawns on our train chugging away to hiking country in Switzerland. Also, there was a muted overhead light at the entrance, discretely illuminating a long, ascendant flight of stairs, which somehow enhanced the mystery of the place.

Having been vetoed by one of our friends, as not likely to dance on tables or suchlike, Joan, Dorothy and I persisted until we became owners of shiny *Maxim's* membership cards. After all this expectation, we found to our disappointment that the clientele was as ordinary and everyday as that found in the Floral Hall on the city's outskirts. Very middle class.

All the girls looked as we did: pretty dresses, shining hair, bright pink lipstick. I hated pink! And pink was all the rage that year. The boys, all clean shaven, wore suits or grey flannels, indistinguishable tweed jackets, and ties selected primarily for decorum by their Mammys. We girls in our pinks lined up across from the boys in their greys. Each sex looked the height of respectability, eerily quite uniform, and definitely not exciting.

In other words, Maxim's held no surprises and was not half as much fun as the familiar plain Floral Hall on the city's outskirts, which in turn hardly held a candle to Hall's Hotel in the rural town of Antrim.

Nevertheless we went. Girls did in Ireland in those days — in groups or twos. To go to a dance with a boyfriend was almost downright dull, but to go with your girlfriend left one open to the expectation of a Mr. Right or at least a Mr. Maybe. We three often danced or sat the night away at Maxim's, feeling somehow that we were in the midst of un-married, searching Belfast. Mostly, like everyone around us those days, we all smoked. Girlhood, to me, was seen through a companionable haze of blue smog. We never found anyone, but one evening stands out in my mind like a beacon. It all began this way.

The week before we had been hiking in the Mourne mountains, striding over heather-clad hills while the sun shone fitfully. Our final day out, we were so desirous of returning with a tan that we lay between the potato rills (so that the cold winds didn't touch us). For languorous hours, the sun glowed upon our upturned faces. We arrived home as brown as berries, the envy of our city friends. Alas, my hair, instead of bleaching in the sun as Dot's and Joan's did, had become as wispy as hay. "What am I going to do?" I wailed. "We're going to Maxim's on Saturday night!" Out came our *Women's Own* magazine. By God's good luck, the beauty section told us, step by step, what to do with hair "dried by the kiss of the sun."

After shampooing as directed, I heated the prescribed olive oil and rubbed it carefully into my scalp and tresses. Then I heated a towel and sat, ensconced in it for a full hour. I then shampooed my hair again, not once, not twice, but three times. Still I looked like an oily grease spot. Dot and Mammy gazed in horror. "Yer hair's stickin' to your head; ye look a right sight," Mammy said.

"Go out with that hairstyle an' you'll have a parade after ye." Dot looked at me, combed my short hair close to my ears, and swirled a curl in the middle of my forehead. "You're like Betty Boop! Actually, it's made you look a Latin type." I gazed into the mirror. Dot was right.

Two hours later I sidled into Maxim's in the lowest-necked turquoise sweater I'd ever knitted, having developed the courage to wear it for the first time only that night. With it, I wore a tight black skirt, high heels, purple lipstick, and enough mascara on my eyelashes to give the appearance of spider-legs gone crazy. Dot and Joan hung back to see what effect I might have.

I had barely stopped at the edge of the dance floor when a fella I'd always had my eye on (but who had never glanced my way), tapped me on the shoulder and said, "I've never seen you here before. Are you from around here?" I batted my eyelashes at him, nearly blinding myself in the process.

"How cleever av yoo. I am not from here. I am Italiana. I am from ze Imperial City of Roma," I purred. Handsome Harry's eyes gleamed as he took me in a determined clinch, swept me into a foxtrot and breathed, "I just love those films you folk make." I smiled as if I had run them up myself on a sewing machine. He had all the intentions of pasting me to his body for the rest of the night, but he never had the chance.

Bemused, my sister and Joan watched as at every dance I was whirled into the gaiety of quick steps, waltzes and fox trots by boys they had longed to dance with and by boys whom I had longed to dance with. The news had flown round the grapevine that there was a real live foreigner in their midst. The only good thing about my popularity was that I was able to repeat the same small talk with every one of them. "I am from Roma. Belfast was beutif-ool. The Eye-talian marbles in the city Hall were fan-tas-teek. The men in this city are ver' 'ansoom."

I made these remarks, even the last one, to the ugliest of Belfast hellions. Guess what? They drank it in! They swaggered, they straightened their ties, and they swung me round in fancy steps they would never have tried with a Belfast native. And what was I doing through all of this? The olive oil slowly trickled down the back of my neck, so I was mopping ever so discreetly. Mopping and wiping the oil from my neck and my forehead, where it slowly descended from my Betty Boop curl. I prayed that my mascara was not making greasy crow's feet around my grey eyes. One partner had, in a fit of flattery, usually unknown to the Belfast male, described my plain Irish eyes as "grey pools of mystery." This, while he was clutching me in a slow waltz.

Like Cinderella, I pointed in feigned horror at my watch. "I mus' gooo," I said to the latest glazed-eyed romantic. "In Roma, giiiirls must go home earlee." I waved in the direction of a muscle-bound Rugby type, big and beefy and absolutely innocent. "My brother Luieegee, he awaits." I made for the door where my sister and Joan were doubled up with laughter, just as the strains of "Jealousy" engulfed the dancehall. An enormous plump young man with a red face and hair the color of a dandelion puffball caught me by the wrist and said "Not so fast, this one's for me. You can't say no to a Latin dance."

"But a tango ees Spanish, me I am...." "I know, dearie," he said, "an' you're from Rome, but just wait." With these simple words, he cleared the floor in front of us. The music swelled, my feet flew, and the notes were one with my breathing, my steps, my pauses, my turns…. Perfection. There was no conversation, there was just me, and the dance, and the music with a partner whom I have never forgotten as long as I've lived. All I lacked was a rose between my teeth. I said "yoo were queet wunnerfoo!" and really meant it as I wiggled my way out of the door and turned to wave a truly heartfelt thanks.

"Loved it dearie," he mouthed and gave me a big coarse wink.

In the cloakroom Dot and Joan helped me into my coat. "Where could he have come from?" I asked as we rattled down the stairs. "He must be a gigolo," said Dot (who being four years older knew these things). "Nonsense" said Joan, "He more than likely dances at the Plaza six nights a week."

"I don't care where he learned to dance," I said dreamily. "Fancy me, dancing the tango. I'll never forget it." I think you'd better get back to your young farmers at Hall's Hotel," Joan said briskly.

"Aye, and the Military Two-step instead of tangos," Dot added.

"I suppose you're right," I agreed. "I needn't think of showin' my face round Maxim's for a couple of months in case some of those fellas who made eee-jits of themselves twig on to me playing a trick on them." I twirled round on the square sets on Castle Street, "but just for one night it was bloomin' marvelous to be from Roma, ze Imperiaaal Citee.

A FRIEND OF MY FATHER'S

During the Second World War my father, who was a member of the R.U.C. (the Royal Ulster Constabulary in Northern Ireland), spent most of his days, and oftentimes nights, at the entrance to the Belfast Harbor Commission, perusing with solemn dignity all cars and identity cards which moved back and forth in that military-inspected zone. It was a serious job. But to us, his two wee daughters, such work was fraught, not with peril, but with stories of adventure and humor, with which he would regale us nightly.

One of his most popular tales was about a man with whom Daddy worked. His name was William Dynes, but throughout our childhood he was known as "Stinker" Dynes. We would wheedle our father into telling us of Stinker's latest escapade. Without the use of his favorite adjective, these recitations would have been normal, if not downright dull. In reality, this is the kind of monologue Daddy would retell:

> "Augh hello Billy," sez Stinker Dynes to me,
>   comin' in the backdoor of the nissen hut down
>   at Sydenham "Isn't it one stinkin' coul' day, and

am I stinkin' well starving from standin' all the livelong day until my stinkin' feet are stinkin' well frozen to the stinkin' puddles on the stinkin' pavement. An' just as I was thinkin' of nippin' round the stinkin' corner to yon wee stinkin' widder woman till have a sup of stinkin' char, than who do you think stinkin' well hoves intill stinkin' sight, but the stinkin' Rajah hisself [a nickname for a most feared Sergeant on the police force]. So I just had to put such stinkin' thoughts out of m' stinkin' head, and get back to m'stinkin' points duty."

Such long spiels of invectives would make Dorothy and me curl up and roll with glee on the carpet. Daddy would beam upon us, well pleased at amusing his wee daughters so easily.

Time passed, and the year I turned nineteen our father died. As is usual in Ireland "the remains," as we fondly call the dead body, were laid out in the back bedroom, and my sister and I were kept busy answering doorbells, pouring strong tea, handing round ham sandwiches and receiving effusive sympathy. The house was full of grieving relatives and friends, discussing everything from what favorite won on the 3:30 race to the fine character of the dear departed. Without warning, the doorbell's shaky whirr was once again heard throughout the house. I hurried to answer, smoothing down my gray woolen dress and adjusting my facial features to show bereavement as I opened the door.

Standing on the cement step, wearing a too-long raincoat and turning a stained paddy hat between nervous red hands, was a little man with white hair and a devout face. I bowed slightly in greeting, and the man moved hesitantly forward saying, "You won't have heard of me Miss Kerr, but I used to work with your father during the war. My name is William Dynes."

I had an overwhelming desire to shriek, "Welcome Stinker Dynes, centre of long tirades of fatherly recitals, welcome, and a thousand times welcome!" But, instead, I placed my young hand in his old one and said, "We are most pleased that you had the time to visit us on this sad occasion; would you care to view the remains?" Sedately, we climbed the stairs.

CHRISTMAS
STORIES

A CHILD'S CHRISTMAS IN ULSTER

Christmas always started out with smells. For what seemed like weeks beforehand, an aroma of cinnamon, ginger and brown sugar greeted me at the kitchen door when I slammed home from school. "Can I have some, Mammy?" I would ask. Back would come the stock reply, with almost a tinge of piety about it, "Augh no, darling! 'Sure you know it's for Christmas." Thus yet another batch of maid-of-honors, current squares, or German biscuits, bejeweled with silver balls and pink sugar candies, would be popped into some large tin. The lid would always be crammed tightly shut with yards of greaseproof paper. "Ye must keep the air out," she would admonish, "so as to keep the freshness in."

In those years, in the early 1930s in Belfast, we had little money, but the two little daughters of Constable Kerr never knew. We would laboriously write out our Christmas lists. After we had finished them *really neatly*, our father would read them over *he said* to make sure our handwriting was perfect. Then he would carefully light both corners and holding them over our coal fire we would watch, completely entranced, the crinkle of grey ash being wafted up the chimney by the high draft. There, we were told, Father Christmas (for that's what we called Santa Clause in Ireland) would catch them, and if we were good little girls (here a kindly shake of the finger), we might have some of our wishes granted.

Five days before Christmas my Mother would take me down to the Holywood Arches, our marketing district. There she would haggle between Lemon's the fowlman and Thomson's Fancy Fruit, not only for a turkey but for two holly wreaths. How I loved to be given the job of carrying our prickly purchases home, safely strung on my small arm. We would walk up the hill with a faint skiff of sleet clinging to our tweed coats. The gas lit street lamps were shimmering in a pale mizzling haze, leading us up, up into our tree-lined avenue. The wreaths were not for our doors. What! Waste money on us — never! They were to show love and respect to our dear departed. Later in the week, Mammy with at least three of her sisters would travel over to the City Cemetery and lay the wreaths on their parents' graves. How red the berries shone beside the glistening holly leaves. Somehow I compared these circlets with Christ's crown of thorns and the berries with the blood on his forehead, which I had gleaned from fervent study in my Sunday school book, *Gospel Stories for Little Wanderers*.

Christmas Eve would not have *been* Christmas Eve if my sister, Dorothy, had not vomited with excitement. Looking down all the cornucopia of years, I can still remember my poor sister, who normally was a most level-headed child, spewing up in the bathroom, with my Mother saying "Why do you let yourself get in such a state?"

Yet, year after year, until I was twelve, I remember Dot clambering over my little body saying, "Oh Margaret, I feel I'm going to be sick," and she was. Then she would return to bed and we would cuddle under the quilts, arms around one

another. I would ask, "Better now?" as if I were the older sister
and she the younger, instead of the other way about. Finally
we would fall asleep to the sound of the carol singers from
Bloomfield Presbyterian Church, sounding like the very angels
they were singing about:

> *While angels watched their flocks by night*
> *All seated on the ground*
> *The angels of the Lord came down*
> *And glory shone around.*

And there we lay, wrapped not only in sleep but also in
twisted flannel sheets which, on that night, strangely resembled
swaddling clothes.

CHRISTMAS 1939

Every Christmas of my childhood, come Hell or high water, my mother — short of money all the rest of the year — managed to collect a jarful of change. Every year, mother's crockery jar held enough so she could take my sister and me downtown to Robb's at Castle Junction — one of the best family stores in the City — to visit Father Christmas.

The particular year that comes to mind, though I didn't realize it at the time, was the year that war had been declared that September. People spoke of it as "being over by Christmas," but of course it wasn't. That Christmas was the prelude to many years of scarcity to follow, when our city was blacked out at night in case of enemy bombers, shops were no longer well stocked, and their once bright, decorated windows were boarded up in case of bomb blast. However, as children, we were not aware of what was to follow.

So, that December, our pleasure was heightened by the fact that Aunt Aileen Murphy had decided to bring her two sons with her. This meant that six of us, all dressed up in our best clothes, were hustled downtown. We loved our cousins, Morrell and Derek, so there were no happier children in Robb's that day.

The children's toy department on the top floor was patrolled by a nervous, brittle man whose nose could have easily cut cheese. His manner was highly deferential. Seeing, at a glance, that we were not of the crème de la crème of Belfast society, a smile of supercilious superiority flitted across his features. He bowed — slightly — murmuring, "No doubt these young ones have come to visit Father Christmas?" Upon our mothers combined rhythm of nods, he pointed out the paper-streamered way to the grotto. At least that was what we expected, but that year the well known, slightly shabby blue cave had disappeared and instead of Santa and his Elves, we were thunderstruck to behold a tall white arch to "The Good Ship Fairyland."

In we all trooped with Auntie Aileen saying "Oh Lord May, I hope it doesn't rock too bad or I'll be sick." Mammy, her elder by eleven months retorted, "Now Aileen, houl' your tongue, and don't upset the children's enjoyment." We tiptoed in. The ship was lit with small bulbs, by which we could dimly decipher seats ranked along each side like animals in the ark — two by two. Gingerly, Dorothy and I sat down, carefully arranging our skirts over our knobbly knees, as good little girls had been taught to do in a city where Victoriana still reigned supreme. Derek and Morrrell immediately plunked down behind us, but the mothers hastily sent them packing to the other side of the vehicle, "as you never know what mischief those four'll get into when the boat starts." We four scowled at the grownups.

Slowly the boat began to pitch, rock and toss. The lights brightened a little and a voice overhead (like God himself, I thought) informed us that this was no ordinary boat, but in actual fact, a submarine, which would soon be taking us through the marvels of the deep. "Look out for the great conger eel" boomed the voice, and suddenly, outside the little portholes there was an eerie green light and fishes small and gigantic solemnly wobbled by. We were thrilled. We saw a cruel conger eel and an overfed mermaid with much seaweed around the upper portion of her body, but with a splendid tail, and then slowly our vessel stopped. A door at the far end opened unto the most splendid shining grotto of all time. Plum in the middle of it was a Father Christmas to surpass all Father Christmases; big of belly, hearty of voice and — oh the presents! They were heaped in piles around him.

"Do you think he'll give one to me?" squeaked Derek, who was only four and having had his adenoids removed recently, spoke between grunts, wheezes and a four foot long striped scarf. "Of course," said Dorothy, who at twelve, knew everything there was to know. Hesitantly the mothers shepherded us towards this important personage.

Each of us was given a neatly tied parcel covered in white paper. Then we felt ourselves ushered, rather quickly, through another door which led, surprisingly, to a back stair in Robb's.

Soon we were on a swaying tram with our noses pressed against the windows, watching all the shops flashing by — some with turkeys and hens hanging outside or with holly wreaths for Christmas gravesides. People would swing unto the tram and chuck us under the chin and ask with beer-laden breath, "An' who's the lucky wee lassie who's been to see Father Christmas today?" Dorothy and I would smile shyly and clutch our packages. When finally the tramstop hove in sight, off we tumbled (the children, not the mothers), hurtling ourselves over the road, which in those days of horse and cart traffic (and only an occasional bouncy car) was as safe as our front room.

After our tea (and leaving our long-suffering mothers washing up the dishes in the scullery), we were finally told "You may now open your presents, you've been right good the day." Morrell and Derek both had jig-saws and Dorothy a rug-making kit, but when I opened my square, flat box there was nothing in it but lots of tiny round balls on a cardboard star. The balls were in different colors, rather like the iridescent quality of butterfly wings. However, I didn't know what to do with them, as there was no list of instructions. I took my box to the mothers who chorused, "Augh darling,' we don't know, but aren't they pretty?" I hastened to Uncle Albert, who had been gassed in the trenches in the First World War, had been near to death, and was therefore looked upon as almost an oracle in the family. He surveyed the little balls and the star-shape, and then with a slight cough, he shook his head and shrugged his shoulders. "I never saw the like of them in my life before."

That night I played behind the sofa with the colored balls and listened to the grown-ups interesting gossip. I arranged the balls in long lines, I made lovely kaleidoscopic designs. I shook some into the star-shape to see how many I could get into the holes. I even tried to snuff some up my nose, but Morrell and Dorothy stopped that, though Derek appeared interested.

I kept the game intact for years. I never discovered what it was until I came to live in America some twenty-five years later. It was Chinese Checkers, so I bought a box for my children, and although there was a list of instructions we didn't need it as my husband had played the game "for always." Ken was surprised that I didn't know it, in the same way as I was amazed that he didn't know "Snakes and Ladders."

A rocking vessel, Christmas, and warmth of family are as crowded in my thoughts, as those colored balls that tantalized my mind by their beauty and mystery all those years ago. They were like the beginning of girlhood, so full of loveliness and wonder, secret symbols and obscurity. In a funny way, I wish I hadn't found out what they were. For now, in old age, I understand that, for me, the mystery of the unknown game

was irrevocably mixed with the enchantment of a trip by rolling
submarine through the unchartered seas of green seaweed and
flipping-tailed mermaids to a land of fir trees and snow as thick
as icing-sugar on a bridal cake, and a wonderful gleaming world
of happy-ever-afters.

CHAPTER EIGHTEEN

LEST WE FORGET

Once upon a time there was a time when I had nothing to do at Christmas except be there. I did not have to pluck the turkey, stir the Christmas pudding or bake for five solid days beforehand. Neither did I have to weep copiously, at least twice, because something had fallen flat that should have risen, or risen like a mountain when it should have been as flat as a billiard table. Yes, there really were those days, and I shared them with my friend Eileen Kelly.

The Arches was our shopping district in east Belfast then, deriving its name from arches that supported a prominent nearby railway bridge. The bridge — and the rows of shops — were located at the foot of the hill from our neighborhood. Eileen Kelly and I would press our noses to windows down at the Arches and talk about all the lovely things we would like for Christmas, well knowing that none were for us. Eileen's poor father had been a chronic invalid for all of the nine years I had known him and my father was a policeman, earning the princely sum of $14 per week. This reality did not stop their small daughters from dreaming. When my handsome sailor cousin, Norman Crothers, a petty officer in his Majesty's Royal Navy, invited us to go shopping with him in the city, our minds sprang to the unlikely hope that "perhaps he'll buy us something." Unfortunately, I shared this thought with our Mother before we left. She was horrified. "Sure young Norman hasn't the money to be squandering it on you two wee hussies." She wiped a strand of hair back as she peeled the potatoes and reiterated, as I skipped out the door, "Remember if he does offer you anything, be careful to think of his wallet."

Eileen and I sat on each side of Norman, not knowing what to say. Eileen had dimples, so she dimpled prettily. I didn't, so I just hung my brown wool stockings over the edge of the seat and hoped that he'd offer to buy me a book. I loved books and nobody ever gave me one, except the Greys of Dunmurry, who sent me one every Christmas. I daydreamed, *Wouldn't it be marvelous if Norman allowed me to choose a book?* So as my delicious friend Eileen twinkled up at my cousin and accepted the tram tickets when the conductor punched them, I sat solemnly, wishing that I were not in two halves. You see, one side of me was saying, "Gee, you could pick a wonderful adventure book with ghosts and murderers." Meanwhile the other side, the Band of Hope, Christian Endeavour part was saying, "Stop this minute! I must remember what Mammy said and not choose anything! Or if I do, it must be cheap." No wonder I frowned. It was very difficult to be a child in Belfast in the early 1940s.

At any rate, when we finally reached town, Norman helped us off the tram and asked us to help him choose something nice for his girlfriend, Maureen. We loved doing this; so much so that we totally forgot ourselves. We were dazzled by the jewelry, the soft pretty clothes and were somewhat surprised when he wheeled round at the escalator. "Seeing you were such a couple of bricks helping me to buy Maureen's present," he said, in his English-accented Belfast voice (he'd left our city years ago), "let's go upstairs to the Toy Department."

Well, you could have knocked us down with a feather. Eileen and I stole little glances of greed and delight at one another. Our dreams were going to come true after all. As we entered the portals, my guardian angel hissed in a most unlady-like fashion "not expensive, remember what Mammy said." Norman led us toward the counter.

In the middle of the room was the most splendid railway set with stations, flashing lights, bridges and villages, through which chugged a stalwart shining train marked The Golden Arrow on the side. We dutifully stopped and watched, as Norman was so interested (Fancy! At twenty four years of age, I disdainfully thought). What our eyes had lighted on were dolls and doll house furniture.

Now you must understand, at that particular time there was not a feminist bone in our little bodies. We loved dolls. Soft, cuddly and sweet. We loved dolls that said "Ma Ma!" in a weird bleating tone, had eyes that opened and shut, or had eyes that stared straight ahead. We just plain loved dolls. However, the year before I had received my pride and joy, a minute doll house, with a front that swiveled out on hinges to disclose four tiny rooms, somewhat sparsely and poorly furnished. I, of course, did not know that at the time. But when I saw what was on Robb's counter that day, I realized that my furniture was mere utility in comparison to the plush, cushioned chairs, the metal standard lamps, the graceful chaise lounge and a darling sewing basket with petite scissors.

As I was gazing at this collection labeled "For the Drawing-Room," I felt Norman's eyes upon me. Quickly, I seized a box of terrible gimcrack furniture in brittle poor wood and croaked, "Oh, this is lovely Norman, I'd like this one." Norman took the box out of my hand and gently laid it down. "No, Margaret, Eileen chose the doll she wanted, so you must take this one."

He picked my first choice. "No, No,' I squeaked. I had noted that it cost nine shillings and sixpence. Why, that amount could buy three books. That was a sinful amount! But when I looked up into Norman's eyes and then back at the box in his hand, my eyes filled with happy tears and I nodded speechlessly.

"Kindly erase the price off both gifts," Norman said. I breathed a big sigh of relief. "I'll tell your Mum it cost five shillings," he whispered. He and I smiled like conspirators.

Eileen hugged her doll, while I swung my package tied with a red ribbon. The three of us marched down the stairs of Robb's, spurning the clanking escalator. We felt like rich stars in a movie. I longed to do some fancy tap dance, like Shirley Temple, but we just jumped the last two steps.

In the New Year Norman returned to duty. By springtime he was reported "missing in action, presumed killed" in one of the great North Atlantic battles.

I never really knew him. He was so much older than me, yet something told him that day that he wanted to buy the best for two little girls who had never received "the best" before. We, who had been brought up making do with what was offered to us, had our first taste of walking into the finest toy department in the city and choosing exactly what we longed for. It was a heady, wonderful feeling, and I still remember it clearly, and with deep, lasting thanks.

CHANGE OF SEASON

When I read Frank McCourt's *Angela's Ashes,* I was struck by the opening words, "Worse than the ordinary miserable childhood is the miserable Irish childhood, and worse yet is the miserable Irish Catholic childhood." I could have wept for him. You see, I came from the *other* side of the fence. We Kerrs were a Protestant family. My father's one generation in Ulster Scottish clan warred with my Mother's native Irish side, not by fists, drink or hard words, but by their sanctity, musicality (Daddy's two sisters played the piano) and their strict religious views on everything under the sun.

Dot and I — and our cousins — were reared as Scottish Presbyterians. Three times to church on Sunday, our parents marched us in full Sabbath regalia every weekend to see and be seen by all the church-going flock of East Belfast. How did we bear it? We had to learn not only the hymns and Bible verses by heart, but even the psalms. Today, this may sound like cruelty to children. In our early years, it was the normal way of life. Later I wondered if our suffocating upbringing was the reason that Dot and I almost fell backwards trying to be good.

Still, we were who we were. By the time Dorothy and I reached our rebellious teens, we were straining at the leash. The first thing we did was break away from the Christmas celebrations, held by the Walkers, the Irish side of the family. Daddy's family hardly took that holiday under their notice, but held Hogmanay, Old Year's Night, with singing and jollity at Grandfather Kerr's.

Dot and I refused to partake of the usual festivities. "No, we don't want to go to Aunt Aileen's on Christmas Day. No we don't want to go dancing on Boxing Day." We shook our heads. We didn't want to do what we'd always done.

"So then what *are* you pair goin' t' do?" wailed our poor Mother.

"We're off to the mountains to spend our days hiking. We'd rather have canned soup or baked beans. "Food!" we snorted, "Who cares about food?" We cooked on a primus stove in youth hostels where we sat around pot-bellied stoves with like-minded malcontents.

"But what will your Aunts, Uncles and cousins think?"

With a chorus of, "We don't care, we don't care," we were off towards the Mourne Mountains, our boots big, our rucksacks bigger, and scowls on our young faces. We wanted *our own life*.

Of course we did; we enjoyed our freedom. What young person doesn't? But, naturally, after a certain length of time and travel, of living away from home, we began to be nostalgic about Christmas.

"Remember how the Aunts squabbled in the kitchen," Dot said. "I told you, Aileen, to drain those potatoes fifteen minutes ago and now they're mush!" "Don't give our Margaret too much plum pudding or she'll be sick; it is very rich." "Where the Hell — I mean heck — did I put the large platter? I had it a minute ago."

I joined in. "Do you remember how they would all blow up at Aunt Lily? 'Lily get out from under our feet, you're standing there with your two arms the one length doin' nawthin!'" My sister and I giggled.

"Poor Aunt Lily," Dot said. "She always sat in Uncle Albert's chair next the fire, and everyone would yell at her to get up and give the poor man his seat." At that time we didn't know that he had been gassed in the First World War, and was our family hero.

"The part I loved about Christmas," I said, "was sitting round the table with all our cousins. We always had something to laugh about. And of course Aunt Aileen's recitations were wonderful. Christmas wouldn't have been Christmas without them. Remember "The Mistletoe Bough," and how it scared all of us youngsters?" Dot and I decided to go home. We could barely wait for the plane to touch down at Nutt's Corner.

Parents, Aunts and rosy-cheeked cousins hailed us with love and affection. Nobody kissed. People didn't in our families. But their faces, older now by many years, glowed with welcome. This time, we set the table without being asked. Aunt Lily sat in Uncle Albert's chair because he had died the year before. To our astonishment, Aunt Evie now wielded an enormous canteen teapot, almost as big as herself. "Aye, we decided three years ago we needed a bigger pot. It saves me trottin' back and forth to the kitchen, so we all planked money down in order to buy a good one." She beamed at us. "So good to have you home." This time, instead of serving the younger folk first at a secondary table, all generations sat at one table together. The boy cousins were no longer with us; they were at their girlfriends homes. We missed them, but the meal was as good as ever. I ate a full serving of plum pudding without feeling queasy.

Dot rolled up her sleeves and I took up the drying towel. Seeing us wash up the dishes, Mammy and the Aunts seemed relieved. With so many plates, butter dishes, serving bowls, pots and pans, the new kettle was kept on the gas stove for innumerable rinses. "We'll all be in the sitting room," Aunt Vi called, "come in when you're ready." I so looked forward to the sight: Aunt Lily in Uncle Albert's chair, Aunt Vi handing round a big box of chocolates, Aunt Aileen refusing them because of her weight, Mammy and Uncle Nelson (our one remaining Uncle) smoking like railway trains on the sofa, and everyone cajoling Aunt Aileen for one of her recitations. We hung up the drying cloths, placed the plates back on their shelves and hurried in.

The scene was not what we expected. *Silence* greeted us. Everyone was seated in their usual place, but now each held a flat white card in their hands. Aunt Vi handed us similar cards. On each card were rows of numbers.

For the next two hours, until our Mother and we left to catch the trolley home, we played — you guessed it — Bingo. Wee Aunt Vi (not quite five feet and a great leader of modernity) had introduced the family to the game. We learned that "clickety-click" meant 66 and "Legs Eleven" was always said when 11 came up. Aunt Vi supplied little prizes for the winner of each game. I came home with a dishmop and Dot with a bar of smelly soap, while Mammy won a packet of Gallaher's Blue, her favorite cigarettes. "Wasn't that the greatest fun?" Mammy asked. "Trust our Vi to discover something new." Dot and I withheld our groans.

On the plane back to Edinburgh Dot and I were finally able to vent our true feelings. We'd told the family it had been great fun, and wonderful to be home for Christmas — all true, as far as it went. "I think that was why the cousins weren't there," I surmised. Dot agreed. "I guess we'd rather have Christmas BC rather than Christmas BB" Dot said. I looked blankly at her for a second and then we both shrieked "Before Bingo." Several passengers glared at us, but we, being in our twenties, thought we were hilarious.

TWO GIFTS

I swear before my Maker that some of the best things that happen in life appear out of the blue. They may be a fluke, a mishap or an unexpected gift. It was the latter with me. When I arrived in this country with not a friend in sight, my mother-in-law, Mim, handed me a big heavy parcel. When I opened it I found it was *The American Woman's Cook Book* and although I wasn't an American nor much of cook either, when I saw on the flyleaf "Good Eatin' from Aunt Bertha and Uncle Henry" I was deeply touched. It was a wedding present.

"Who are they?" I asked, "We must go and thank them personally." Mim, looking a little flustered. "They're farming folks, Henry is the cousin of Grandpa Peirce and we haven't visited them in twenty years." Then she added, like the knell of doom. "They're Quakers."

"Great! So was my Welsh grandmother," I beamed.

"Why don't you send a note of thanks?" Mim said, but that was not my way. Ken and I visited them at their farm a few days later. A cow barn sat on a rise, a fancy cupola on top. Did the cows appreciate to be in such a fancy building, I wondered? Our cow byres in Ireland were much simpler affairs. The barn sat near a low lying farmhouse, neat and tidy, its every window sporting white lace curtains at a similar angle. Beyond the lawn was a field of tall corn. Just off the road — on the corner of their front lot — stood a sturdy shed whose sign offered preserves, corn and green beans. A crooked cardboard notice advised shoppers to "Sound Horn" for service. We rolled into the circular driveway. Little did I know that this was the beginning of my great friendship with Aunt Bertha, originally from Lancashire and thirty years my senior.

Everything about her I loved. She always wore a flowered apron in the house. Aunt Bertha's grey hair, caught back in a tiny bun, wisped round a face that held boundless kindness, and blue eyes brimming with playful humor which she used on Uncle Henry daily. Her mate was as skinny as she was plump. Faded blue bib overalls hung loosely on Henry's slight frame. His cantankerous character was apparent that first day as he warned us to discuss no religion or politics in his house. "Oh don't go on so, Henry" Bertha said! "They've come for *apple pie."* Her baking was legendary in the area, but I would have gone to the farm if she'd served crusts.

Over the years, I learned her history. How she, her mother and sister had followed their father to the cotton mills in New Bedford. They sailed into Fall River on a Sunday night and she was working on the mill floor the following morning. The year was 1919. I often asked her for stories or remembrances of that time. Her answer was always the same, "Eeh, Ah don' reetly remember." However, she taught me how to hook rugs from woolen rags, old coats, skirts and the like, and that made all the difference.

When I am hooking a rug, I sing all the time, even now when my voice is somewhat rusty and I cannot reach the high notes. With Aunt Bertha, rug hooking set her tongue and her memory free. Finally, one winter's day in her sunny kitchen, long after Henry had died, as we sat companionably with our hooking frames cocked up in front of us and our hooks flashing, she told me the following story:

"Henry, far from being rich, had really nothing but the farm, which brought in little. Oftentimes, with the three children coming close on one another, the purse could be almost empty. We always had food on the table, living on a self-supporting farm. I always had the kitchen steamed up with canning vegetables and berry preserves during the summer. As for extras," she gave me a rueful laugh, "Well, there was precious little. Yet, you know, a woman, even working on a farm and with children at school, does need to get out and visit occasionally. So there was this day…." She smiled and lowered the rags she had been cutting to her lap.

"Do you remember Ida Corey? She lived near to Ken and his parents. Well, she was the President of the Fairhaven Ladies Benevolent Association. When she drove up in her big blue Chevy one day, telling me that there's going to be a grand Christmas Party in the Benevolent Hall on New Boston Road, I was delighted. She asked me if I could bring a custard pie and maybe an apple cobbler. Ida Corey was always awful bossy, told you what to do and bring, though she never brought anything herself you understand. She was a very good organizer; I have to give her that. Of course I agreed readily." Aunt Bertha paused in her story, inhaled deeply, lowered her chin and smiled sheepishly. I nodded in ready agreement.

"'Good!' says Ida Corey, the organizer personified, 'I'll collect you at noon and bring you back,' and with that she swings the big Chevy round the driveway. Then, just as I'm turning into the doorway, she suddenly grinds the car to a halt, winds down the window and peals halfway across the farmyard so that half the neighborhood could hear, 'Bertha, I forgot, be sure to bring a small gift for under the Christmas tree. We are all bringing one gift and taking one gift home with us.' And off she trundled, leaving me with a black cloud hanging over my head. *If I had known* that there was to be a gift as well as the eats, I would have made some excuse. What in the world could I afford to give as a present? All I had was my egg money and that was for the essentials. I was beside myself, you can well imagine."

I nodded in sympathy. "So what did you do?" sez I, well knowing that Aunt Bertha would have thought of something.

Aunt Bertha hunted for a bit of dark green cloth, hooked in a leaf in the right hand side of her rug and stopped, hook poised for effect. "I'm tellin' you, I could think of nothin'. I was flummoxed. But up I goes to the attic and looks in the trunk where I kept my old flour bags. I brought out three and then I rummages in my mother-in-law's old bedroom, for I remembered she was a grand hand at embroidery. Sure enough, I found some wee bits of embroidery silk: green, red, and some gold thread. The dear soul, she'd been dead for years then, had carefully placed all of these in a box with a sliver of soap to keep the moths away. Down the stairs I came, right into this very kitchen, and started bleaching those flour bags straight away."

"We've got to have a good cup of tea." Bertha suddenly said, "I'm right dry with all of this gabbin." She picked up the fat round teapot, warmed it and picked up the gently simmering kettle on the cast iron stove, opened her cookie jar for one large lemon cookie each, and then settled down to continue. I poured out the milk, heaped a teaspoonful of sugar in each cup, and sat waiting for the tea to brew. When I filled our cups it was with strong brown liquid that would have curled your hair. We sipped contentedly. I nibbled my cookie and said, through crumbs, "So what?"

"Well, you understand, I had to do any extra work only in the evening, when everything else was seen to. Henry would milk the cows, and I would see to the vegetables we grew, make the meals, make sure the children's homework was done. But by gum, I found time to bleach those flour sacks, until they were as white as the fallen snow. I cut the bits of coarse fabric into a full apron shape and sewed it on the machine that's now in the living room with the overflowing spider plant on top of it. You know the one I mean?" I nodded. "I sewed that apron with good long ties, you know the kind that are so long you can wrap them twice around the waist so that the children won't come behind you and undo them." Her eyes glowed as if she'd made a great joke. "The demons!" She smiled at the memory and then continued. "It looked better than homemade, I must say. I was pretty pleased with it, though I knew it was only begun. I had yet to embroider it, so that it would be fancy, fit for a Christmas gift." Aunt Bertha sighed deeply as if remembering the task that still lay ahead.

"Thank Goodness, I had some red and green ric-rac for above the hem. Then I drew, as best I could, candy canes, a poinsettia, and a snowman — the usual festive symbols on the skirt of the apron. Finally, on the pocket, for you must have a pocket on an apron, it's a necessity, I outlined a candle and its flame with the glittering gold thread. I'm tellin' you, by the time I had stitched, embroidered and hemmed everything, it looked a proper treat. Forgive me for sounding proud! But then, oh my dear, how pride comes before a fall! I discovered that not in the length and breadth of the house was there one scrap of Christmas paper to be found.

Every bit of Christmas paper from the year before that I'd saved and carefully ironed was wrapped around the children's gifts at the foot of our tree in the parlor. I was at my wit's end. The next day was the party. So guess what I did? *Guess what I had to do?* I folded my lovely apron carefully in the only paper I could find — brown kraft paper — and tied the whole thing up with a scrap of thick green and red yarn I happened to have. Looking at it, honestly, it looked like a pound of liver. I thought of how brightly wrapped other ladies' boxes would be. You can imagine how I felt."

I roared with laughter. "It was no laughing matter," Aunt Bertha said.

The next day, with Ida Corey calling for me, I hid my poor parcel between the two pies in my basket. I prayed that Ida Corey wouldn't ask me what I'd brought. Luckily she was too busy telling me what her Clarence was going to buy her for

Christmas. We arrived safely at the Ladies Benevolent Hall without me having to say a word. I crept in and hid my brown paper parcel in the back, behind all the glorious red, green, silver and gold Christmas paper packages under the tree.

All the women were dressed up, many in dresses made just for the season. I was so glad I'd pinned my mother's gold broach on my best frock, the one with white swirls. We had a lovely meal: turkey, dressing, squash casserole, mashed potatoes, corn, green beans, fruit and berry pies of every description, and our choice of tea or coffee. You know what? I could hardly eat a bite for worrying about the gift-giving.

Sure enough, Ida Corey looms up in the middle of the room, hardly before we'd eaten our desserts. Then she starts ordering us all, one at a time, to take an under-the-tree present "as a token for what Christmas and our friendships mean." All I could see, with the parade of women, was that *nobody* was choosing mine. All the ladies were opening their packets. You can imagine what it was like: soft filmy scarves, sensible knitted gloves, the odd bit of jewelry, and boxes of chocolates. All around me, ladies were crying with joy and exclaiming with every opening. My brown paper parcel was still visible at the back. It lay by itself, alone, like a lost soul.

"Well now," says Ida Corey, "has everyone got?" "Not Bertha Pierce," Fanny Babbitt my dear friend, called out. I could have murdered her on the spot. Ida Corey looked slightly put out. In a moment, she sighted the red and green yarn at the back of the tree and pounced on my humble gift. She stood victorious and proclaimed, "There you are, Bertha! There's one for you after all."

"Now you understand, everyone had already opened their parcels, so naturally all eyes swiveled toward me and my pathetic brown paper package. Tut-tuts of sympathy came from corners of the room. *What had poor Bertha Pierce been left with?* Slowly, I undid the bow. Hesitantly, I peeled away the stiff brown butcher paper." Aunt Bertha paused for a sip of tea. As she cleared her throat, a sly smile of delight flickered across her sweet face. "I shook out the paper and unto my lap cascaded my-white-as-the-driven-snow apron, gleaming in red and green symbols of Christmas and with the candle on the pocket sparkling. There was a *gasp* all over the hall as I held up my apron for all to see."

I rocked back and forth with delight, my chair almost knocking over my hooking frame. Aunt Bertha hooked a full row of her rug, then resumed. "They all wanted to exchange with me. 'I'll give you my scarf or jewelry, or chocolates,' they said, and then, in the next breath, 'Who made such a beautiful thing?'"

"I said, 'I did.' The voices clamored all the more. 'Change with me Bertha,' they cried. But I just said 'No, No, I'm going to keep it for myself,' for I thought they shouldn't have judged a book by its cover." Complacently, she snipped at a violet and yellow pansy in her rug. "I kept it and wore it until the embroidery faded and even the gold of the candle flame was snuffed out by the years."

Bertha and I smiled at one another. I shook my head in admiration. Rug-hookers and friends, thirty years apart but close in heart. I use the dog-eared, somewhat-smeared from over-use *American Woman's Cookery Book* to this day.

READING
GROUP
EXTRAS

BIOGRAPHICAL NOTE

Born in 1931, **Maggi Kerr Peirce** grew up with an abiding love of red brick factories and the sonorous moan of the foghorns out on the lough. She has since lived in Stockholm, Amsterdam, London and Edinburgh and came to the USA in 1964. By 1967 she was director of the Tryworks Coffee House in New Bedford where she coaxed her young folk to turn to a love of traditional music and song. Before long, she was asked to take part in various folk festivals in Canada and America as a singer of Northern Irish pastoral songs. One thing led to another. Recitations, stories and songs had been part of her upbringing. She shared everything. Among many libraries, schools, etc. she has performed at Folk Life on the Mall, the Smithsonian, the Mariposa Folk Festival near Toronto, Ontario, National Festival at Wolf Trap, Philadelphia Folk Festival, Prairie Home Companion and Jonesborough Storytelling Festival. She lives in Fairhaven, Mass. with her husband Ken and one snooty feline.

QUESTIONS POSED TO MAGGI KERR PEIRCE AND HER ANSWERS

MARCH, 2013

Q **Your Mother was very different, wasn't she?**

A Yes. She tried to mold us to her shape but we were not at all like her. She was difficult to live with which is very Irish. Daddy was rather sober. We children often giggled uncontrollably, listening to them from behind the kitchen door. Sometimes you saw flashes of spirit in mum, but mostly she wasn't well or particularly happy. I loved her and I must say I have written several poems about her, whereas only one about Daddy. There's a message there somehow.

By the way, neither of my parents ever said "I love you" to either Dot or me — not in our whole life. Still, we *knew* and didn't need paltry words. Daddy would tug my hair as he passed by and Mammy would say "Awa' wi' y'" if I dared to ask. As Dot and I grew up, we became so different from mum. She would have really loved us to have worn white shoes and hats and gone to church every Sunday and done "the right thing".

Q **You never said where you'd actually worked in a Chocolate Factory?**

A Dot and I did actually work in a chocolate factory, but it was anything but a sweet experience. The factory was in Sweden, not too far from the International Youth House where we lived. Inside, the factory was spotless, but lifeless, too. You could eat anything and everything your heart or stomach desired while inside the building, but you were forbidden to take anything out. However, there was one time, I think it was for St. Patrick's Day, Dot and I decided to have a party. We determined to get chocolates out of that place if it was the last thing we did. I baked soda and wheaten bread. Chocolates would make the celebration complete. We had dungarees with a little bib pocket, so every day for weeks we filched three chocolates a day, put them in our bibs and sauntered on home. Everyone at the party enjoyed them immensely. Dot and I disliked the factory as it was very boring, and we lost all taste for any kind of chocolate for many years.

Q **Do tell us more about your father. He sounds quite a character.**

A No, he wasn't really. Or perhaps he is only in retrospect. He was a very quiet, straight as a die kind of man. He ran away from home at 14 and joined the army. He hated the army but learned some Boer War songs and lots of First World War ditties while he was there. His Mother (bless her though I never knew her), paid his way out of the army. Then he then went off and joined the Royal Navy, which he adored. We even called our wee semi-detached house in Belfast "Wahine" after his old ship. That was how much he loved it. Mammy threw out all the pictures of it at his death. Thanks to a naval friend of ours in Maryland, I now have photos of the Wahine. I just wish my dear sister had lived to see them. Daddy was Irish but his upbringing (I now realize) was totally Scottish. He was handsome. I know all little girls think their Dads are dashing, but our father really was a smasher.

Q **It's so funny to realize that you were first and foremost a folksinger when you first performed. How did that happen?**

A Dot and I had always sung together. When we travelled we learned songs in Sweden, Holland, Germany. Then when we moved to Edinburgh, Scotland, a very old friend of ours, Hamish Henderson, a renowned folklorist, heard that we had arrived. He invited us to join a Folksong Society just them being formed at the Edinburgh University. We became founding members quite by chance. Somewhat to our annoyance, Dot and I discovered that people would rather hear our pastoral folksongs and Belfast street songs than any of our German or Dutch ditties.

Q **How did you actually come to America?**

A While in Scotland, I married a Unitarian from Fairhaven Massachusetts. We married in Edinburgh, Scotland, at St. Mark's Unitarian Universalist Church. We moved to his hometown in New England, where we have been ever since. If I had married an Englishman I'd have lived in England.

If I'd married a Dutchman I'd have lived in Amsterdam. It was as simple as that. I had no particular interest in America, strangely enough. Honestly, I thought that I would live in Edinburgh to the end of my days. It just shows you what happens when you say "Never."

Q So what did America do for you?

A That's a rough question for you're going to get a straight
answer. Moving from Ireland to small town Massachusetts
was very difficult for me. Strangely enough, when you are
going through travail — and that's what I went through
for several years here — you find strength and comfort in
unexpected places. At first, I could not settle down. We had
two babies. I was so lonely it was torture. My travail lead me
to two events that changed my life. First, I learned to hook
rugs from Ken's grandfather's cousin's elderly wife, who we
called Aunt Bertha. Second, because of my loneliness I was
thrown back, thought-wise, to my early days. In the memories
of my childhood, I found comfort. Remembering the places
— mum's kitchen, Daddy's big chair — was comforting.
Everything from bringing into my mind's eye the Mourne
Mountains and the winding, rock-strewn path up to the
heights, to the songs I sang as a child and young girl brought
relief. Grief can lead to many good things. I remember
reading a Chinese proverb once which went "I may live
on until I long for this time in which I am so unhappy and
remember it fondly." It's true, but I wouldn't want to go back.

Q But I meant: who discovered you over here?

A I do remember singing at a round robin group at the Newport Folk Festival. A lovely man called Frank Warner and his dear wife, Anne, turned out to be renowned collectors in the 1950s. I think Appalachian music was their prime interest. Frank liked a song I sang at Newport, one of the few Irish famine songs I sang there, and we talked. The Warners became good friends of mine, as did their son Jeff, himself a great traditional singer. Then, running the Tryworks Coffee House in New Bedford, I became known as a singer. I have an ordinary voice. I'm no soprano but I don't go flat. Anyway, it was the words I was always interested in.

Q You've told stories at the well known National Storytelling Festival in Jonesborough, Tennessee. How did you arrive there? Did you send a tape or such?

A I met the famous kissing cousins, Barbara (Freeman) and Connie (Regan-Blake) at our local Eisteddfod in 1978-79 and in 1980 when I was in Bethlehem, Pennsylvania, trying to learn German script writing (and failing miserably), I suddenly received a phone call from them asking me to come to Jonesborough for a storytelling festival. I said "What's a Storytelling Festival?" I'd never heard of the like. However, I had told stories from the early 1970s — in all kinds of places — from the Smithsonian Folklife Festival on the National Mall to Dominican College in California and the Puppet Theatre in Syracuse. The National Storytelling Network, the membership association of ethnic and professional storytellers in the USA has given me their Oracle Award for Lifetime Achievement, so I've been very blessed.

Q **When you returned to Ireland from Europe,
what kind of work did you do?**

A My sister Dot returned to the Drawing Office at Harland
and Wolff's as she had asked for time off. I, however, had
left a hideous job in an Insurance Office and was glad to see
the heels of it. Still, I went back to office work. Because a girl
who had been hired to do shorthand and typing had refused
the job, I stepped into it. I stayed there seven years, loved
the work and ended up Assistant to the Sales Manager. After
leaving the Insurance Company at age fifteen, I learned to
leave a job within two weeks if I didn't like it. My Mother
taught me that after the misery of working in the Insurance
office.

Q **How do you feel about storytelling in the family?
Do you think people have time for it during these
busy days?**

A I feel that this still takes place. We all had stories before we
went to bed. They maybe were tiny stories, or continuing
sagas that never ended. I found car journeys a natural time
for songs, conundrums, stories of childhood or made up
stories. Also, ordinary chatting over the debris of a dinner
table — that is if you plan to eat one meal all together once
a day — perfect times for what they did, what teacher said,
what Dad or Mom saw today. Start the ball rolling.....

Q What changes have you seen with societal storytelling?

A I find storytellers too often go the easy way. They tell nothing but amusing stories. I am not against stories that make for laughter, but I have always felt that stories were a connecting time, and life is not one big joke. We know that. Do we not want to face it? Do we not want to hear that uneasiness reaching up from the audience?

GLOSSARY

'bee's knees'	(43)	Expression for "all that," or the ultimate
'broth of a girl'	(75)	A waif
Country yins	(65)	Country folk
Electric power house	(36)	Electricity generating plant
Ethel M. Dell	(22)	Actress known for the melodramatic roles in which she excelled
Dhoti	(61)	A piece of apparel which supports an affectation
Dinned	(31)	Beaten or worked into one's awareness through repeated emphatic repetition
Fag-ends	(79)	Cigarette butts
Farls	(51)	Flatbread cakes
Fitted carpet	(44)	Wall-to-wall carpeting
Fringe	(18)	Hair falling over the forehead, i.e.: "bangs"
Fountain pen	(23)	A writing instrument popular during the 20th Century
Great Depression, the	(10)	Historical period during which most national economies were characterized by insufficient jobs for laboring people, insufficient capital to promote growth
Hard boiled sweets	(45)	Hard candy

Hemstitching company	(13)	A business where women worked stitching and ironing garments for the ready-to-wear trade
Knickers	(18)	Throughout the UK, underpants are known as "knickers."
Liberty bodice	(18)	A camisole-like undergarment for women and girls that replaced corsets during the early 20th Century
Linen houses	(10)	A business where linen garments are manufactured
Marzipan	(23)	A confection consisting of almond paste and sugar
Midges	(63)	Flying insects commonly mistaken for mosquitoes
Napoleon's Nose	(9)	A rock prominence visible from Belfast
Points duty	(54)	Traffic-directing police duty in the intersection in Dublin called "the points"
Poppycock	(12)	A colloquial expression for nonsense
Oxter	(11)	Archaic term referring to the underarm
Quare	(51)	Irish dialect term for unusual, strange, remarkable
Retroussé nose	(27)	A turned-up nose, very fashionable at the time
Romany	(82)	Gypsies or those who live nomadic lives
Ropeworks	(9)	In the era prior to cellophane tape, twine was a major packaging item, and for a harbor city like Belfast, boats and ships required rope suppliers.

Royal Ulster Constabulary	(10)	Ireland's domestic police force at the time
'scarce as hen's teeth'	(18)	Expression emphasizing scarcity
Scittery gits	(30)	"Scittery" shares a common root with "scat," a term for feces. "Git" was a term from Ireland of the time referring to a waif, an unkempt young woman.
Sheugh	(50)	Ditch, trench, or swamp
Skivvy	(35)	A waifish young girl
Shipbuilding	(9)	A business at which boats and ships are constructed or repaired
Sixpence	(18)	Money, a British coin
Thon	(65)	Equivalent of "that yonder"
Tramfare	(19)	Fare for a ride on the tram, or intracity train
Tufty	(30)	Hair billowing in small bunches
Wean	(28)	Archaic term for an infant or young toddler